Financial help for families
What you need to know

Child Poverty Action Group

Published by Child Poverty Action Group
30 Micawber Street
London N1 7TB
Tel: 020 7837 7979
staff@cpag.org.uk
cpag.org.uk
© Child Poverty Action Group 2020

A CIP record for this book is available from the British Library.
ISBN: 978 1 910715 69 7

Child Poverty Action Group is a charity registered in England and Wales (registration
number 294841) and in Scotland (registration number SC039339), and is a company
limited by guarantee, registered in England (registration number 1993854). VAT number:
690 808117

Cover design by Colorido Studios
Internal design by Devious Designs
Typeset by DLxml, a division of RefineCatch Limited, Bungay, Suffolk
Content management system by KonnectSoft
Printed and bound in the UK by CPI Group (UK) Ltd, Croydon CR0 4YY

Note: the benefit rates in this book are those that apply in 2020/21 and may change in
future years.

Authors
Mark Brough is a freelance writer on welfare rights.
Alison Gillies is a welfare rights worker at CPAG in Scotland.
Kirsty McKechnie is a welfare rights worker at CPAG in Scotland.
Simon Osborne is a welfare rights worker at CPAG.
Ed Pybus is a welfare rights worker at CPAG in Scotland.
Frances Ryan is a welfare rights worker at CPAG in Scotland.
Angela Toal is a welfare rights worker at CPAG in Scotland.
Mark Willis is a welfare rights worker at CPAG in Scotland.

Acknowledgements
Many thanks are due to Sabrina Dubash, Kelly-Marie Jones, Judith Paterson, Jessica Strode and Gary Vaux. Also to Nicola Johnston for her thorough editing and for managing the book's production, Anne Ketley for compiling the index and Pauline Phillips for proofreading the text.

About Child Poverty Action Group

Child Poverty Action Group is a national charity that works on behalf of the more than one in four children in the UK growing up in poverty. We use our understanding of what causes poverty and the impact it has on children's lives to campaign for policies that will prevent and solve poverty – for good.

We provide trusted and expert information and advice for the welfare rights and advice community – online, and through our books, training and advice services. Our advice lines support thousands of advisers a year, helping them to give families the best information and advice. Our *Welfare Benefits and Tax Credits Handbook*, described as the 'adviser's bible', is used by Citizens Advice, local authorities and law centres throughout the UK. We also keep advisers up to date with trends and changes in the social security system through bulletins and our highly regarded training courses and seminars.

Poverty affects more than one in four children in the UK today. When children grow up poor, they miss out – and so do the rest of us. They miss out on the things most children take for granted: warm clothes, school trips, having friends over for tea. They do less well at school and earn less as adults. Any family can fall on hard times and find it difficult to make ends meet. But poverty is not inevitable. With the right policies every child can have the opportunity to do well in life, and we all share the rewards of having a stronger economy and a healthier, fairer society.

If you would like to join us to help end child poverty, please visit cpag.org.uk, or follow us on Facebook (facebook.com/cpaguk) and Twitter (@cpaguk).

Keeping up to date

You can get the latest information on benefits by booking on a CPAG training course. We can also provide your workplace with in-house training. See cpag.org.uk/training for more information.

Our *Welfare Benefits and Tax Credits Handbook 2020/21*, published in April 2020, tells you all you need to know about entitlement to benefits and tax credits. Visit cpag.org.uk/shop to purchase a copy.

With up-to-date information, insights, decision-making tools and appeal-letter generators, AskCPAG is our online platform that supplements the expertise advisers have come to trust and rely on from our rights handbooks and training. AskCPAG provides digital access to our flagship *Welfare Benefits and Tax Credit Handbook*, which is fully searchable and updated throughout the year online. See AskCPAG.org.uk to subscribe or find out more.

Getting advice

Your local Citizens Advice office or other advice centre can give you advice and support on benefits. See citizensadvice.org.uk if you live in England or Wales, or cas.org.uk if you live in Scotland.

CPAG has an advice line for advisers.

For advisers in England, Wales and Northern Ireland:
Telephone: 020 7812 5231, Monday to Friday 10am to 12pm and 2pm to 4pm.
Email: advice@cpag.org.uk (for enquiries about universal credit, child benefit and tax credits only).

For advisers in Scotland:
Telephone: 0141 552 0552, Monday to Thursday 10am to 4pm and Friday 10am to 12pm.
Email: advice@cpagscotland.org.uk.

Contents

Chapter 1
Support for families

This chapter covers:

1. Why are families struggling for money?

2. What financial support is there?

3. What does this guide cover?

4. Do you work with families?

5. What can you do to support families?

6. Asking about money and debt

What you need to know

- Many people do not claim all the financial support to which they are entitled.

- Getting a benefit check can make a real difference to household income.

- Delays and problems with benefits can leave people without enough money for essentials.

- Getting help to appeal benefit decisions and to access local discretionary financial support can help overcome some benefit problems.

- If you work with a family with money worries, you can support them by referring them to the support and advice they need.

1. Why are families struggling for money?

More than one in four children in the UK are living in poverty. For parents, this means not having enough money to buy essentials and sometimes having to make difficult choices between buying food for the family and paying bills.

Families may struggle for money when they work fewer hours than they would like or when wages are low. They may struggle for money when they are out of work or not able to work. The coronavirus pandemic has impacted many parents as their pay was reduced or they lost their jobs.

Family incomes do not stretch as far as they used to. High housing costs, childcare costs and fuel bills make it harder to manage. To keep pace with rising household costs, the rates of social security benefits used to increase every year in line with the cost of living. But in recent years, for most family benefits, this did not happen. So for most families who get a social security benefit, it is harder to make ends meet.

What families say

Making ends meet

'I say to the kids, "Tonight, we'll light candles, and we'll get our books in bed." And it's because I've no electric. And when I've run out of gas and there's no hot water, we'll boil kettles for the bath. I don't tell the boy – who's only 12 – because I don't want him panicking and thinking, oh my god, my mum hasn't got any money.' *Mother of a disabled child*

'I can't go and buy them stuff that they need, when they need it, if you ken what I mean... like trainers and things, they're just so expensive. I think I'm quite lucky, my family are brilliant... because obviously Christmas is in December and their birthdays are in June, like my mum and all that will buy them clothes and trainers and things for their birthday, and that kind of lasts them until Christmastime, and then they'll do the same... And that will kind of keep them going until June, until their birthdays. And then come their birthdays, they'll give them money or go buy them an outfit each... and that will do them until Christmas again.' *Lone parent*

Benefits are available to help families, but many people do not know what they are entitled to. When people do claim benefits, some experience delays or problems that can cause their income to fall or stop suddenly.

There are also changes that are currently being made to the benefits system that affect some families more than others, leaving them worse off. Throughout this book we have included some real-life examples from CPAG in Scotland's 'early warning system' project, which was set up to monitor and analyse the impact of the changes on children and their families.

- **Lone-parent families.** Almost half of children living with one parent live in poverty – nearly twice the rate for children living with two parents. Lone-parent families are expected to be more affected by the changes to the benefits system than two-parent families. This is because lone parents are more likely to claim benefits (as they are likely to have a lower household income from work) and because benefits are likely to make up a higher proportion of their overall income.

- **Families in work.** Families who are in work but who have a low income often get universal credit or working tax credit to top up their earnings. Changes to the rules for these benefits mean that fewer people are now able to get help, and the amount of help is lower.

- **Families with more than two children.** Universal credit and tax credits include amounts for children, but not usually for a child born after 6 April 2017 if there are already two children in the family. So families with three or more children may struggle for money.

Making ends meet

'I've always tried to protect him... So he's not affected by how my income is or how things are for me. He does pick up on when I'm stressed. He can see that. He senses that all the time. He's always like, "Are you okay? You okay?"... The only thing I can do is be honest with him about everything, as honest as I can be, and reassure him that everything is fine. If he sees that I am down, he thinks it's his fault.' *Lone-parent father of a disabled child*

'My oldest was in the kitchen, making a cup of tea or something, and I came in with this bag, and I started taking out the tins, and he was looking at the tins, all stuff I wouldn't buy. And he was like, "What, have you been to the food bank? Are things that bad that you went to the food bank?" Laughing. And I looked at him, and he knew with me looking at him that he was right. And then he went, "Oh my god, is it really that bad?"' *Lone-parent mother*

'If I were to get [my son] here in the now, he would laugh about it and say, "I can't remember the last time mum made a good meal." But I've never told him it's because I can't afford it.' *Lone parent and carer for disabled child and elderly parents*

'I had to go and pick him up from the school one day because he had been sick. Just before lunchtime. He never had any dinner money left. And I said to him, "What's happening? What's going on?" and he said, "I'm getting bullied because I'm poor and I've not got any money for a bacon roll."' *Lone parent*

'I went to the bank on a Monday, expecting just under £300, and there was £86 in my bank. So I thought, "Oh my god, something's came off that, I don't ken what!" And I went to the bank and it was only £86 that had gone in, tax credits. So those weeks I was only getting £86. I couldn't pay gas, I couldn't pay electricity. By the time I put money in my car, and bought the bare essential foodstuff, got school dinners and stuff, I had nothing... I was just at my wits' end.' *Lone parent*

2. What financial support is there?

There are three main kinds of benefits.

- **Benefits to help with living costs** if you are out of work or if you are in work but have a low income. Whether you qualify and how much you get depends on the amount of your income – you must also have no more than a certain amount of savings. These are called 'means-tested benefits'. An example of a means-tested benefit is universal credit. As a condition of getting benefit, you may be given a 'work coach' at the job centre who will expect you to take steps towards getting into work or increasing your earnings.

- **Benefits to help with particular needs**, such as the extra costs of having a disability. The amount you get does not depend on how much income or savings you have. An example of an extra-costs benefit is personal independence payment.

- **Benefits to help in particular circumstances**, such as bereavement. These often depend on your having paid national insurance contributions through work or having national insurance credits. The amount you get does not depend on the level of your income. An example is bereavement support payment.

You can get more than one benefit at once – eg, you could get a disability benefit and child benefit, plus a means-tested benefit to help with living costs.

What is changing with universal credit?

Universal credit is a new benefit that is replacing six other 'means-tested benefits':

- income support
- income-based jobseeker's allowance
- income-related employment and support allowance
- housing benefit
- child tax credit
- working tax credit

Most people cannot make a new claim for these benefits and must claim universal credit instead. If you already get one of these benefits, at some point you must claim universal credit instead.

If you currently get one of these benefits, this stops when you claim universal credit. You usually cannot change your mind and go back onto your old benefit.

The amount of universal credit you get may be different from the amount of benefit you previously received.

Your first universal credit payment is usually made up to five weeks after you claim. If you think you will run out of money, ask the job centre for an 'advance' of universal credit. You start paying back the advance once your normal payments begin.

Universal credit is paid directly into your bank account. You must get a bank account if you do not already have one.

You have your own universal credit online journal. You need to be able to check this regularly, ideally on a daily basis, otherwise you might miss important instructions and could lose benefit. You must set up an email account if you do not have one. Ask for help at your local job centre if you are not confident you can manage online.

EXAMPLE

Claiming universal credit

Emily is a lone parent of school-aged children. She works part time and gets tax credits. She gets a benefit check at her local advice centre. The adviser tells her that she could also get help with her rent. Emily would need to claim universal credit, and her tax credits would stop. The adviser estimates that, overall, Emily would have more money with universal credit. However, to get universal credit, she would probably have to meet a work coach at the job centre regularly, even though she is already working part time.

When you first claim, you may be asked to go to the job centre so that your identity can be verified. You must also agree a 'claimant commitment', containing details of the 'work-related activity' that you agree to undertake. You may have to meet regularly with a 'work coach' at the job centre, although not everyone has to do this.

If you get a benefit check from a local advice agency, ask whether making a benefit claim will mean transferring to universal credit and what this means for you.

What can you do if you have a benefit problem?

Problems do sometimes happen. At the start of a claim, you might find yourself short of money before your first payment arrives. You could have less money than you need to pay your rent. Your payments could be reduced if you miss an interview with your work coach. Whatever the problem, it is best to get advice quickly from a local advice centre. An adviser can give you practical advice, can help you appeal and may be able to suggest other sources of financial support. There is a very good success rate with benefit appeals, so it is well worth appealing if you can.

3. What does this guide cover?

This guide covers all the main social security benefits that you may be able to get for you and your family. It also covers other important financial support, such as child maintenance and help with childcare costs. You can use this guide to find out:

- which benefits you can get when you are having a baby
- how to apply for child maintenance and how much you might get
- whether you can get free childcare or help with childcare costs
- how to get help with school costs, such as clothing, meals and transport
- which benefits you can get if you are out of work or if you have a low income from work
- what you might be expected to do to get ready for work as your children get older

- how benefits can help with your rent or mortgage
- what help is available if someone in the family has a disability
- which benefits to claim after a bereavement
- how benefits are affected if a child goes into care
- the benefits available for foster carers and kinship carers
- how to deal with benefit problems
- what financial help is available in an emergency

When you have identified the help that is available in your circumstances, you can find out more about how to claim and how much you will get in the A to Z list of social security benefits in Chapter 11.

4. Do you work with families?

Our research shows that parents are often anxious about telling people that they have money worries, which may mean they do not seek help and support. A family may be more likely to open up to someone they are used to working with and trust, rather than someone they have never met before. This is why it is important that everyone who works with families feels confident asking about money worries and can help families make contact with the help and support they need. You do not have to be a benefit expert to do this.

5. What can you do to support families?

- Refer your client for a benefit check. This can make a real difference. For example, did you know that even when benefits are limited to two children, there is still extra help for disabled children worth up to £400 a month?

- Refer your client for an energy check. This could reduce the amount the family is spending on energy bills.

- Help families deal with debt. Debt advice could reduce the amount the household is spending on debt repayments, and budgeting advice could prevent a family from getting into debt in the first place.

- Make an application for emergency financial support (known as local welfare assistance) from the local authority.

- Ask the Department for Work and Pensions for an advance of the first payment of benefit. There is often a wait of two to five weeks for the first payment of benefit. If someone has made a new claim for a benefit, but has not yet been paid, s/he may be able to get an advance if there is serious risk to her/his family's health and safety. The advance is recovered from future payments of benefit.

- Ask for a benefit decision to be looked at again. If someone thinks that a benefit decision is wrong, s/he can ask for it to be looked at again within one month of the decision. In some circumstances, a late request can be accepted within 13 months – eg, if s/he has a good reason for not having asked earlier.

- Apply for a discretionary housing payment. Local authorities can make discretionary payments to people to cover shortfalls in their rent.

Has someone been sanctioned?

- Help to avoid a 'sanction'. People who have to look for, or prepare for, work in order to get benefit must usually sign a 'claimant commitment' agreeing the steps they will take. If they do not meet their obligations, they can be sanctioned and their benefit reduced. It is important that the claimant commitment contains any information about the circumstances that may limit someone looking for, or accepting, work – eg, if s/he is looking after a child outside school hours.

- Ask for the sanction to be looked at again. If someone thinks that a sanction decision is wrong, s/he can ask for it to be looked at again. It is important to avoid a sanction if possible because any further sanction period will be longer.

- Ask for a 'hardship payment'. If someone has no money because her/his benefit has been reduced due to a sanction, s/he can apply for a hardship payment. This is a partial refund of the amount of the sanction. Hardship payments of universal credit must be repaid from future payments of universal credit.

What can your service do?

If you work for a service that has contact with children and/or families, it is worth taking time to consider whether there is more you could do to make sure your service is as accessible, easy to use and useful to low-income families as possible. Steps to consider might include the following:

- Is there a Freephone number?

- Could you pay travel costs in advance?

- Is your service open at times that coincide with public transport?

- Are there hidden costs attached to using your service? For example, if you provide free childcare, are families expected to cover the costs of snacks, materials or outings?

- Do you have working links with local advice or income maximisation services? Could you develop these links and develop pathways to directly refer families?

- Do staff know about sources of emergency financial support?

6. Asking about money and debt

Asking clients about money can feel awkward, but it is important that you feel confident to do so. Often people will try to hide their money worries and they may feel too embarrassed to ask for help. Thinking ahead about how you will raise the subject will help you to do it confidently.

Be alert for things that your client says that may indicate possible money worries, but make asking about money worries part of your routine enquiries. That way, you avoid singling out people who may consider there is a stigma attached to being assessed by a professional. It also makes sure you do not miss anyone who might benefit from advice.

Ask opening questions, such as:

- 'Children can be so expensive. Do you find it difficult to make ends meet?'
- 'Do you have any debt?'

Using positive language, reassure your client that help is available:

- 'Advice services can check that you are getting all the benefits you are entitled to.'
- 'Benefit decisions can quite often be wrong. Advice services could double check that decision for you and support you to challenge it if need be.'

Once you have asked your client about her/his money worries, you need to help her/him get the advice and support s/he needs.

'Signposting' means you give your client details of an advice service and your client takes responsibility for making contact.

A 'referral' means that you contact the advice service and get the process of making an appointment underway.

Clients are much more likely to engage with an advice service following a referral than if they have to make contact with the advice service themselves. You will need to be aware of the advice and support agencies locally.

Developing a good-quality referral system between your service and advice services improves access to quality advice and support which can help maximise families' incomes and help prevent or alleviate financial crisis. A 'gold standard' referral system would be universal, or near universal, allowing referrals for anyone who has a low income or money worries of any kind. In addition, it would not rely on action from the parent – the appointment with the advice service would be made as part of the referral, and if this is not possible the parent would be contacted directly by the advice service to make an appointment.

Further information

Benefit checks or support to ask for a decision to be looked at again:
You can find your local Citizens Advice office at citizensadvice.org.uk.
Some local authorities have their own welfare rights service. Check on your local authority website.
Many housing associations have a welfare rights service for their tenants.
Online benefit calculators can give you an idea of what benefits you could get: gov.uk/benefits-calculators.

Questions about benefits and tax credits:
CPAG provides advice to frontline staff working with the public.
In England, Wales and Northern Ireland: 020 7812 5231 or advice@cpag.org.uk. Email advice is limited to queries about universal credit, child benefit, child tax credit and working tax credit only.
In Scotland: 0141 552 0552 or advice@cpagscotland.org.uk.

Energy check:
The Energy Saving Trust: energysavingtrust.org.uk/about-us/contact-us.

Debt advice:
National Debtline: nationaldebtline.org
StepChange: stepchange.org

Housing advice:
Shelter helpline: 0808 800 4444

Who to contact about different benefits:
Universal credit, jobseeker's allowance, income support and employment and support allowance: see gov.uk/contact-jobcentre-plus for the relevant phone number.
Disability living allowance and personal independence payment: see gov.uk/disability-benefits-helpline for the relevant phone number.
Tax credits: see gov.uk/government/organisations/hm-revenue-customs/contact/tax-credits-enquiries for the relevant phone numbers.
Child benefit: see gov.uk/government/organisations/hm-revenue-customs/contact/child-benefit for the phone number.
Housing benefit and local welfare assisstance are delivered by local authorities. Find your local council at gov.uk/find-local-council.

Chapter 2
Having a baby

This chapter covers:

1. What help is available?

2. What help can you get while you are pregnant?

3. How are your benefits affected if you are pregnant?

4. What help can you get when your baby is born?

5. Are you a young parent?

6. Are you adopting a child?

What you need to know

- Do not miss out on support to which you are entitled – get a benefit check as soon as possible after you find out that you are pregnant, and again once your baby is born.

- Tell your employer or 'work coach' at the job centre that you are pregnant.

- Make sure you know your rights at work.

- If you are a young parent, find out whether you can claim or whether your family can claim for you.

- If you are adopting a child, you can qualify for the same, or similar, financial help.

1. What help is available?

Among all the things to consider when you are having a baby, money is likely to be high on the list. Your maternity period is a time when you may experience a reduction in income if you are in work, and an increase in spending, whether you are in work or not. There are some payments and financial help available to you in these circumstances to support you during your maternity period, and help you prepare and provide for your new baby.

Box A

Financial help if you are having a baby: checklist
- free vitamins
- Healthy Start vouchers and vitamins, or Best Start foods in Scotland
- Sure Start maternity grant, or Best Start grant in Scotland
- help with NHS costs
- statutory maternity pay or adoption pay
- statutory paternity pay or shared parental pay
- maternity allowance
- universal credit
- child benefit
- child tax credit (if you already get tax credits)
- Scottish child payment (if you live in Scotland)

2. What help can you get while you are pregnant?

When you find out you are pregnant, it is worth getting a benefit check as soon as possible to make sure that you do not miss out on anything to which you may be entitled. Your GP, health visitor or midwife may be able to refer you to a local advice agency.

Being pregnant, at least in the early stages, may not make any immediate difference to your financial circumstances. You are not automatically entitled to any additional cash payments just because you are pregnant.

Free vitamins

If you live in Scotland (and in some health authorities in England and Wales), you can get free vitamins during your pregnancy. These are provided to all pregnant women, regardless of their income. Ask your

GP or midwife. In other areas, you can get free vitamins if you qualify under the Healthy Start scheme.

Healthy Start vouchers and vitamins

The Healthy Start scheme in England and Wales can help towards your food shopping. Healthy Start vouchers are worth £3.10 a week. You get one voucher during pregnancy, two vouchers per child aged under one and one voucher per child aged one to three. The vouchers can be used at registered retailers to pay for milk, fruit, vegetables and pulses. The scheme also provides free vitamins during pregnancy and your baby's first year, and for children from six months to four years. You can qualify for the scheme from when you are 10 weeks pregnant and until your child's fourth birthday.

Box B

What can you spend your Healthy Start vouchers or Best Start food payment card on?

Healthy Start vouchers and the Best Start food payment card can be used for milk, fruit, vegetables and pulses.

Milk must be plain cow's milk and can be whole, semi-skimmed or skimmed. It must also be pasteurised, sterilised, long-life or ultra-heat treated (UHT), or infant formula milk suitable from birth. You cannot spend your vouchers on flavoured milk, coloured milk, evaporated milk, condensed milk, goat's milk, soya milk, vitamin-enriched milk or other powdered milk.

Fruit and vegetables must be fresh, frozen or canned, with nothing added to them, such as fat, salt, sugar or flavourings.

Pulses, such as beans, lentils and chickpeas, can be fresh, dried or canned, with no added fat, salt, sugar or flavourings.

The Best Start payment card in Scotland can be used for eggs.

If you are not sure how best to use your vouchers, some local authorities or voluntary groups run cookery clubs or parent groups which can help you learn low-cost and easy recipes, and help you get together with other parents.

If you cannot find a registered Healthy Start shop nearby, you can request payments in cash. The Healthy Start scheme may encourage you to approach local retailers and ask them to join the scheme. The government intends to replace Healthy Start vouchers with an electronic payment card in the future.

If you are under 18 and pregnant, you qualify for Healthy Start vouchers and vitamins, regardless of your income.

If you are 18 or over, you can qualify if you or your partner are entitled to any of the following qualifying benefits:

- universal credit (provided your and your partner's combined earned income is no more than £408 a month)
- income support
- income-based jobseeker's allowance
- income-related employment and support allowance
- pension credit
- child tax credit (provided your and your partner's combined income is no more than £16,190 a year and you do not get working tax credit)

You can download a claim form from www.healthystart.nhs.uk/healthy-start-vouchers/how-to-apply. You should tick the box to confirm that you are getting a qualifying benefit; this will be checked with the Department for Work and Pensions or HM Revenue and Customs. It is your responsibility to report any changes in your circumstances.

You can get Healthy Start vouchers and vitamins once you are 10 weeks pregnant, so it is worth applying around this date. You do not have to wait for an ultrasound scan. You cannot get vouchers and vitamins backdated to a date before you applied. If you have applied, and an error is made in issuing the vouchers, you may be able to get a compensation payment. Each voucher must be used by the date stamped on it – this is usually within four weeks but, during the coronavirus pandemic, it has been temporarily extended to within 12 weeks.

Box C
What are Healthy Start vitamins?

Healthy Start women's vitamin tablets contain:

- folic acid: reduces the chance of your baby having spina bifida, a birth defect where the spine does not form properly
- vitamin C: helps maintain healthy tissue in the body
- vitamin D: helps your body to absorb calcium and so supports your baby's bones to develop properly

Healthy Start children's vitamin drops contain:

- vitamin A: for growth, vision in dim light and healthy skin
- vitamin C: helps maintain healthy tissue in the body
- vitamin D: for strong bones and teeth

Healthy Start vitamins are for children aged from six months old or who are having less than 500ml (one pint) of infant formula a day. Babies under six months old who are fully breastfed might benefit from them earlier – ask your midwife or health visitor for advice.

Best Start foods

The Best Start foods payment card in Scotland can help towards your food shopping. Best Start foods payment cards are credited every four weeks, to the value of £4.25 a week during pregnancy, £8.50 a week per child aged under one and £4.25 a week per child aged one or two. The card can be used at all major supermarkets and smaller local shops. If the shop displays the Mastercard logo, you can use your card there. You can spend it on milk, fruit, vegetables, pulses or eggs (Box B). If you qualify for Best Start foods, you should also be able to get Healthy Start vitamins from your health board. You can qualify for Best Start foods from the start of your pregnancy until your child's third birthday.

If you are under 18, you qualify for Best Start foods regardless of your income. You continue to qualify until the end of your pregnancy if you turn 18 while pregnant, or until your child's first birthday if you turn 18 after your baby is born.

If you are aged 18 or over, you qualify for Best Start foods if you or your partner are entitled to any of the following qualifying benefits:

- universal credit (if you earn no more than £610 a month). If you stop getting universal credit, or your income exceeds this limit, you continue to qualify for Best Start foods for eight weeks
- income support
- income-based jobseeker's allowance
- income-related employment and support allowance
- pension credit
- housing benefit and your weekly income is no more than £311
- child tax credit if you are not entitled to working tax credit and your annual income is no more than £16,190
- working tax credit and your annual income is no more than £7,320

You can apply for Best Start foods at mygov.scot/best-start-grant-best-start-foods or by phoning 0800 182 2222.

Sure Start maternity grant

The Sure Start maternity grant in England and Wales provides help with the costs of pregnancy or a new baby (usually only your first baby) if you are on a low income. If you qualify, you are paid £500 in a lump sum into your bank account. It does not have to be repaid. You can spend the money on whatever you think you and your baby need most, and you do not have to provide any evidence of what you have spent it on.

You may qualify for a Sure Start maternity grant if you are pregnant or have given birth in the last six months, and you or your partner have been awarded any of the following qualifying benefits:

- universal credit
- income support
- income-based jobseeker's allowance
- income-related employment and support allowance

- pension credit
- child tax credit
- working tax credit paid with child tax credit or a disabled worker element

You cannot usually get a Sure Start maternity grant if there is another child under the age of 16 in your family, even if you have not received a grant before or if the other child is not your birth child. However, there are exceptions to this rule:

- for multiple births
- if you have your first baby while you are under 20 and you are part of someone else's benefit claim
- if you are a refugee and your older child was born before you came to the UK

If you have a multiple birth and have no other children, you can get a grant of £500 for each baby. If you have a multiple birth and have older children, you can still get a grant but not one for each baby. The number of grants payable is reduced by the number of other children you have from a single pregnancy.

EXAMPLES

Multiple births

Olivia gives birth to twins. She has no other children. She is entitled to two Sure Start maternity grants.

Amira has one child, aged three, and then has twins. She is entitled to one Sure Start maternity grant for the twins.

Eve has twins aged three, and then has another set of twins. She is not entitled to a Sure Start maternity grant for the new twins.

If you have a baby when you are under 16, or under 20 and in full-time 'non-advanced education' (eg, you are at school or college studying for GCSEs or A levels) and you are included in someone else's benefit claim, that person can claim a Sure Start maternity grant for your baby, even if there are other children aged under 16 in the family. S/he must be getting a qualifying benefit and this must be your first baby.

Under 20 year old

Deirdre is 16 and at school. She is pregnant. Her mum, Cathy, gets child tax credit, which includes an amount for Deirdre, as well as for Deirdre's brother and sister, aged 12 and 14. Cathy can claim a Sure Start maternity grant for Deirdre's baby, even though there are other children under 16 in the family.

You can claim a Sure Start maternity grant from 11 weeks before the date your baby is due, and within six months of the birth. If no claim is made within six months, it cannot be paid under any circumstances.

If your child dies or is stillborn after 24 weeks of pregnancy, a grant is still payable, and does not have to be repaid. Chapter 8 has more information on financial help that is available if your child dies.

If you or your partner are waiting to hear about whether you are entitled to a qualifying benefit, do not delay claiming a Sure Start maternity grant. A decision may be put on hold or, if your claim is turned down, you can claim again once a qualifying benefit is awarded.

You can download a claim form (Form SF100) from gov.uk/sure-start-maternity-grant. It must be signed by a health professional, who must also provide the expected (or actual) date of birth and confirm that you have received health and welfare advice. The completed form should be returned to your local Jobcentre Plus office or posted to Freepost DWP SSMG – you do not need a postcode or stamp. The date of your claim is usually the date the completed form is received by the Department for Work and Pensions.

Best Start grant

The Best Start grant in Scotland consists of a payment to provide help with the costs of pregnancy or a new baby, and two more payments in the early years. The pregnancy and baby payment is £600 for your first baby, or £300 if you have another child under 16 in your household.

The money is usually paid into your bank account. It does not have to be repaid. You can spend the money on whatever you think you and your baby need most, and you do not have to provide any evidence of what you have spent it on.

You may qualify for a Best Start grant pregnancy and baby payment if you are pregnant or have given birth in the last six months and you or your partner are getting certain qualifying benefits:

- universal credit
- income support
- income-based jobseeker's allowance
- income-related employment and support allowance
- pension credit
- housing benefit
- child tax credit
- working tax credit

You can also qualify for a Best Start grant pregnancy and baby payment without getting a qualifying benefit if you are aged under 18 when you apply, or aged under 20 and you are a dependant in someone else's benefit claim – eg, your parent is claiming child benefit for you while you are still at school or college studying Highers. You can apply in your own name, regardless of your age.

EXAMPLES

Multiple births

Orlaith gives birth to twins. She has no other children. She is entitled to a grant of £600 for the first twin and £300 for the second twin, plus a £300 multiple birth supplement.

Aileen has one child, aged three, and then has triplets. She is entitled to a grant of £300 for each triplet, plus a £300 multiple birth supplement.

If you have a multiple birth, you get a multiple birth supplement of £300.

You can apply for a Best Start grant pregnancy and baby payment from when you are 24 weeks pregnant, and up to six months after the birth. If you do not claim within six months of the birth, a late claim can be accepted if you were unable to apply earlier due to coronavirus. If your child dies or is stillborn after 24 weeks of pregnancy, a grant is still payable, and does not have to be repaid. Chapter 8 has more information on financial help that is available if your child dies. If you or your partner are waiting to hear about whether you are entitled to a qualifying benefit, do not delay claiming a Best Start grant. A decision may be put on hold or, if your claim is turned down, the decision can be changed if a qualifying benefit is awarded.

You can apply for a Best Start grant online or download a claim form at mygov.scot/best-start-grant-best-start-foods or by phoning 0800 182 2222. It is the same form for Best Start foods and Best Start grant. Remember you can qualify for Best Start foods from the start of pregnancy, and the pregnancy and baby payment from 24 weeks. If you are turned down for a Best Start grant because you have claimed too early, you can claim again when you are 24 weeks pregnant.

Help with NHS costs

You can get free dental treatment and free prescriptions while you are pregnant and within one year of the birth of your baby. All medication and treatment is provided free of charge if you are a hospital inpatient, including around the birth, or while you are an outpatient or at a walk-in centre.

Depending on your income, you may be able to get help with other NHS costs, such as sight tests and glasses, wigs and fabric supports, and fares to hospital for you or your child. You do not have to pay for the cost of these if you or your partner receive certain qualifying benefits or are in an exempt group – eg, if you are a care leaver or an asylum seeker. The qualifying benefits are universal credit (provided your monthly earnings are under £435, or £935 if you have children or a health condition), income support, income-based jobseeker's allowance, income-related employment and support allowance, the 'guarantee credit' of pension credit or tax credits (provided your annual income is under £15,276). If you do not get a qualifying benefit but are on a low income, you may be able to get the item at a reduced cost.

Note: prescriptions, wigs and fabric supports are provided free of charge to everyone in Scotland and Wales. Sight tests and NHS dental check-ups are also free in Scotland.

Are you working?

What the law says

Maternity rights at work

- It is against the law for your employer to sack you or force you to give up your job because you are pregnant.

- You have the right to paid time off for antenatal appointments.

- Your employer has a duty to carry out a health and safety assessment of any risks to you or your unborn baby associated with your job, such as heavy lifting or carrying, standing or sitting for long periods without adequate breaks, long working hours or exposure to toxic substances.

- If there are risks, your employer should take reasonable steps to remove them – eg, by offering you different work or changing your hours.

- If your employer cannot remove a risk, you should be suspended on full pay.

- You have the right to 52 weeks' maternity leave.

- You have the right to statutory maternity pay if you meet the employment and earnings conditions.

- You have the right to return to your job after your maternity leave.

See gov.uk/working-when-pregnant-your-rights

If you are in work, it is usually a good idea to let your employer know you are pregnant, usually at least 15 weeks before your due date, or as soon as you can. You are protected by law and depending on the type of work you do, you may want to ask for your duties to be adjusted.

Statutory maternity pay

If you work for an employer, you may be entitled to statutory maternity pay. This is paid to you as wages by your employer in the later stages of your pregnancy and after the birth, for a total of 39 weeks. Statutory maternity pay is the minimum the law requires employers to pay. You may be entitled to more generous occupational maternity pay, depending on the terms of your contract of employment. You do not have to intend to go back to work in order to qualify for statutory maternity pay, and it does not have to be repaid if you do not return to work.

If you meet the conditions, you have a legal right to statutory maternity pay and your employer is breaking the law if it refuses to pay it. If your employer dismisses you at any time while you are pregnant or after you have given birth, solely or mainly to avoid paying you statutory maternity pay, it is still liable to pay it. Employers can recover some or all of the statutory maternity pay they pay from the government. You may also be able to claim unfair dismissal. If you give up your job, you are dismissed or the job ends after your period of statutory maternity pay has begun, your employer is still liable to pay you until the end of the period.

If your baby is stillborn after the 24th week of pregnancy, or dies, statutory maternity pay is payable for the whole maternity pay period. Chapter 8 has more information on financial help that is available if your child dies.

Statutory maternity pay can be paid for a period of 39 consecutive weeks, starting, at the earliest, from the 11th week before your baby is due and, at the latest, the day after the birth. If your baby is born earlier than the 11th week before the expected week, your statutory maternity pay begins on the day after the birth.

If your employer says that you are not entitled to statutory maternity pay and you disagree, you can contact the HM Revenue and Customs Statutory Payment Disputes Team on 0300 322 9422 to request a new decision.

Your baby's father, or your partner, may also qualify for statutory paternity leave and pay to be able to take two weeks off work to support you and care for the baby.

If you and the baby's father, or your partner, want to share the care of your baby in the first year, you may qualify for statutory shared parental leave and pay. You must take at least two weeks' statutory maternity leave (four weeks if you work in a factory) – you can then decide to give it up for statutory shared parental leave and pay instead. This allows you to divide the leave (eg, taking three months each) or take time off at the same time.

What CPAG says

Working tax credit

If you were getting working tax credit before going on maternity leave or getting statutory maternity pay or maternity allowance, make sure you phone the Tax Credit Helpline on 0345 300 3900 to let the Tax Credit Office know that you are on maternity leave or getting statutory maternity pay or maternity allowance – you are still entitled to working tax credit for 39 weeks in this situation and you can start getting child tax credit when your baby is born.

Maternity allowance

If you have a recent work history but do not qualify for statutory maternity pay, you may be entitled to maternity allowance. This may be payable if you are self-employed, or if you have not worked for the same employer for long enough, or if your earnings are too low to get statutory maternity pay, or if you have recently stopped working. It is not 'means tested' (your income and savings are not taken into account) and it does not depend on your having paid national insurance contributions.

Maternity allowance is payable for a period of 39 consecutive weeks, starting, at the earliest, from the 11th week before your baby is due and, at the latest, the day after the birth. If your baby is born earlier than the 11th week before s/he is due, maternity allowance begins on the day after the birth.

You can claim at any time after the end of the 15th week before your baby is due. You should also provide a maternity certificate (MATB1), given to you by your GP or midwife, proof of having worked and evidence of your earnings. You may need to delay claiming if you will not meet the conditions until later in your pregnancy.

Maternity allowance can be backdated for up to three months. If your employer has told you that you are not entitled to statutory maternity pay and you claim maternity allowance within three months of this notification, your claim can be backdated to the date you notified your employer that you wanted to apply for statutory maternity pay.

What CPAG says

Universal credit

Maternity allowance counts as unearned income in full for universal credit (unlike statutory maternity pay, which counts as earnings, so some of it is ignored). In some cases, especially if you are not liable for rent, getting maternity allowance may mean that your income is too high to qualify for universal credit. This means that you could miss out on other support that universal credit qualifies you for, such as the Sure Start maternity grant and Healthy Start vouchers, or Best Start in Scotland. Get advice to check if you would be better off on universal credit. CPAG is challenging the treatment of maternity allowance in universal credit – for more information see cpag.org.uk/welfare-rights/resources/test-case/maternity-allowance-and-universal-credit.

3. How are your benefits affected if you are pregnant?

Do you have to look for work?

If you have to look for work in order to get benefit, tell your 'work coach' at the job centre that you are pregnant as soon as you can. You can agree restrictions on the hours or type of work you are looking for. You are usually still expected to look for work until 11 weeks before the week your baby is due, unless you have a pregnancy-related illness or there is a risk to you or your baby. You may be able to agree that there are certain types of work that would not be suitable for you – eg, jobs that involve prolonged standing or heavy physical tasks.

If you are claiming jobseeker's allowance while you are pregnant, you must continue to be available for work and looking for work, within limits as agreed. If you are sick during your pregnancy, you may be able to continue on jobseeker's allowance for up to 13 weeks, if you provide medical evidence of your illness.

When you have 11 weeks to go before your baby is due, you usually have the option to stop claiming jobseeker's allowance, so that you no longer have to look for work. This means you can usually make a new claim for universal credit. Chapter 11 explains who cannot claim universal credit.

If you are claiming universal credit while you are pregnant, your work-related requirements might not change for the first 29 weeks, so you may still have to be available for work and look for work, within limits as agreed. You cannot have any 'work-related requirements' imposed on you from 11 weeks before your baby is due until 15 weeks after the birth, or while you are the main carer of a child under the age of one.

If you are claiming universal credit as a couple, your partner must usually still meet all her/his work-related requirements right up to, and after, the birth. However, s/he should notify her/his 'work coach' of when your baby is due and get this recorded in her/his 'claimant commitment'. If s/he fails to meet her/his work-related requirements as agreed because s/he has to be with you suddenly due to your pregnancy or going into labour, s/he should explain this as soon as possible to avoid a 'sanction' being imposed and her/his benefit reduced. Chapter 5 has more information about your work-related requirements.

Switching from jobseeker's allowance to universal credit

Sonia is six months pregnant and is getting jobseeker's allowance. She has already asked for her claimant commitment to be adjusted so that she does not have to look for work that involves standing for long periods, and this has been agreed. However, she is finding looking for work and applying for jobs stressful. When there are 11 weeks to go before her due date, she can claim universal credit and does not have any work-related requirements. When her baby is born, she should report the birth so that she gets a child element for her baby.

Are you at risk of being sanctioned?

If you do not do what you have agreed to do to look for work, there is a risk that you will be sanctioned. A 'sanction' means your benefit is reduced. You can challenge a decision to impose a sanction. A sanction should not be imposed if have a good reason for not doing what was expected of you. A good reason may be related to your pregnancy – eg, if you missed an appointment because you had to get urgent medical attention.

If you are sanctioned while pregnant and claiming universal credit or jobseeker's allowance, you can request 'hardship payments' of your universal credit or jobseeker's allowance. You must show that you are in hardship. You can apply straight away for these because you are considered to be vulnerable due to pregnancy. You must still meet your 'work-related requirements' or 'jobseeking conditions' as agreed.

If you are claiming universal credit, you must reapply for hardship payments at the end of each monthly universal credit 'assessment period'. Hardship payments of universal credit are recoverable, so you must accept that you will have to pay them back once the sanction has ended.

When there are 11 weeks or less before your baby is due, the amount of the sanction in universal credit should be adjusted automatically, so that you are left with an amount of benefit that is equivalent to the amount of a hardship payment. The sanction should not be increased within 15 weeks of the birth, and while you are responsible for a child under the age of one.

Chapter 10 has more information on what you should do if you have been sanctioned, or threatened with a sanction.

Do you have a disability or are you ill?

If you have a disability or long-term health condition, or you become ill during your pregnancy, this may make a difference to your benefit entitlement and what you are expected to do in return for benefit.

Pregnancy, in itself, is not considered an illness, but you may be considered to have a pregnancy-related illness (eg, severe morning sickness), if this is confirmed by medical evidence. Your entitlement may also change if there are complications with your pregnancy which put you or your baby at risk.

If you are claiming universal credit or jobseeker's allowance and are not well enough to look for work, tell your 'work coach' at the job centre. You may be asked to provide medical evidence from your doctor. You are allowed two periods of sickness of up to two weeks in any 12-month period, during which time you are not required to look for work. For universal credit, the Department for Work and Pensions has the discretion to extend this period, or allow more than two periods of illness. For jobseeker's allowance, you are also allowed one extended period of sickness of up to 13 weeks. You still need to be willing and able to take up work when you are feeling better.

If you are not well enough to look for work at all during your pregnancy, you may be able to claim employment and support allowance (depending on your national insurance contributions) without being required to look for work. You may still be required to attend work-focused interviews or prepare for work. You can qualify for employment and support allowance while you are pregnant if you are entitled to maternity allowance, or if you are within six weeks of the date your baby is due or 14 days after giving birth.

If your doctor says there is a serious risk to your health or to your baby's health if you work or prepare for work, you can claim employment and support allowance or universal credit without being required to look for work or prepare for work.

Chapter 7 has more information on benefits for people with a disability or long-term health condition.

4. What help can you get when your baby is born?

Child benefit

You should claim child benefit as soon as you can after your baby is born and you have registered the birth. You can find the claim form in the 'bounty pack' usually given to new mothers in hospital.

Almost everyone with children can get child benefit, although you may not be entitled if your immigration status does not allow you to claim benefits, or if your baby is taken into care. You must be living with your baby or contributing at least the amount of child benefit to support her/him.

You can claim child benefit if you are under 16. Alternatively, if you live with your parent(s) or guardian, s/he can claim child benefit for both you and your baby instead. However, you get £7.10 a week more if you claim yourself, because a higher amount is payable for a person's first child.

If you are already getting child benefit for another child, you must still complete the claim form and fill in the relevant section about other children.

What CPAG says

Everyone entitled to child benefit should claim it

Child benefit is payable to all families, regardless of their income. However, if you have a high income, you may have to pay some, or all, of it back through income tax.

For every £100 of your taxable income over £50,000, you must pay 1 per cent of your child benefit back. If your income is over £60,000, you must pay the full amount of child benefit back as income tax. This rule applies to your or your partner's individual income, not to your joint income.

You should still claim child benefit as it protects your national insurance record by giving you entitlement to national insurance 'credits' that count towards your retirement pension. Claiming child benefit for your child also means that s/he will automatically be issued a national insurance number when s/he turns 16. It is also helpful to have made a claim, so that you can receive child benefit as soon as possible if your income goes down, or if you separate from your partner or you are bereaved. You can claim child benefit and choose not to receive it if you would rather not go through the process of completing a tax return and paying it back through income tax.

You only need to provide a reference number from the birth certificate if the birth has been registered in Great Britain. If the birth was not registered in Great Britain, you must usually send your baby's original birth certificate with the claim form, and it will be returned to you within four weeks.

Child benefit can only be backdated for three months, so it is important not to delay making a new claim more than three months, or you will lose money. It can take up to 12 weeks for child benefit claims to be processed.

When you are awarded child benefit, you are given a child benefit reference number – make a note of this and keep it safe.

Box D
Baby boxes in Scotland

The Scottish government provides a free baby box to all new parents in Scotland, regardless of their income. Some hospital trusts in England and Wales have also introduced baby boxes.

The box contains the following basic items for a newborn baby, worth around £100. The box is also suitable for babies to sleep in:

- mattress
- fitted cot sheets
- satin-edged cellular blanket
- mattress protector
- pramsuit with hood
- all-in-one day suit
- romper and bodysuit set
- scratch mittens
- short-sleeved bodysuit
- long-sleeved bodysuit
- long-sleeved bodysuit with integral scratch mitten
- long-sleeved wraparound bodysuit
- footed leggings
- fleece jacket with hood
- jersey trousers
- baby wrap
- hooded bath towel
- real nappy and liners
- digital ear thermometer and replacement hygiene cover
- natural bath sponge
- bath and room baby thermometer and battery
- dribbler bib
- organic cotton muslin squares
- comforter/soother toy
- PlayTalkRead play mat
- PlayTalkRead travel changing mat
- baby book
- nursing pad

You can get a baby box as well as other help to which you qualify. See parentclub.scot for more information.

Universal credit

If you get universal credit, you may be entitled to an extra amount of universal credit for your baby.

If you are already getting universal credit, you should report on your online journal that you have had your baby. You are entitled to an additional amount (called a 'child element'), worth £235.83 a month. Make sure you tell your 'work coach' or notify the change online or in writing before the end of the universal credit 'assessment period' in which your baby is born. You are entitled to the child element for the whole of that month. If you leave it late, you may miss out unless there were special circumstances that meant you could not notify the birth earlier.

Note: if you are already responsible for two or more children, you may not get extra universal credit for a new baby (see Box E).

If your child has a disability and gets disability living allowance, a 'disabled child addition' is payable, even if the basic child amount is not payable for her/him because of the 'two-child limit'.

What families say

The two-child limit

'Our client has two children and is pregnant with her third child. She wanted to start a family with her new partner and believed that she would be exempt from the two-child limit because her first child was born when she was 15 and would therefore be classed as statutory rape. However, the exemption for children conceived without consent does not apply to the child that is about to be born, and therefore the family will be subject to the two-child limit.' *Local authority welfare rights officer*

Box E

Have you got two or more children?

If you already have two or more children, you cannot usually get a universal credit child element or child tax credit element for a new baby. This is called the 'two-child limit'.

There are exceptions to this rule:

- You have a multiple birth (eg, twins) and have just one other child. In this case, you can get a child element for all the children in the multiple birth. If you already have two or more children, you can get a child element for all but one of the children in the multiple birth.

- You have adopted a child from local authority care.

- You are under 16 (for universal credit) or under 20 and in full-time 'non-advanced education' (for child tax credit) and someone else is claiming universal credit or child tax credit for you – her/his benefit includes an amount for your baby.

- You are not the child's parent, but you have taken responsibility for her/him under specific legal provisions, or you receive guardian's allowance for her/him, or a social worker confirms that the child would otherwise be at risk of being taken into care.

- Your child is likely to have been conceived as a result of rape or a coercive or controlling relationship, and you are not living with the perpetrator.

If you are paying for childcare, you should report your total childcare costs for all your children, as these can be included in universal credit, even if the basic child element is not payable because of the 'two-child limit'. Chapter 4 has more information on getting help with paying for childcare.

The two-child limit

CPAG believes that limiting universal credit and child tax credit to two children is morally wrong. It contravenes the rights of the child and the right to family life, as well as breaching human rights in other specific cases – eg, because of religious or conscientious beliefs about contraception or abortion. If you are affected by the two-child limit in any circumstances, get advice to challenge the decision.

Child tax credit

Child tax credit is a benefit to help you with the costs of supporting a child. It is 'means tested', so the amount you get depends on the amount of income you have, as well as your circumstances. You can start to get child tax credit if you already get working tax credit. You can get an increase if you already get child tax credit for another child. **Note:** if you are already responsible for two or more children, you may not get extra child tax credit for a new baby (see Box E).

In most cases, you cannot make a new claim for child tax credit and must claim universal credit instead.

Chapter 11 explains who cannot claim universal credit.

If you are already getting tax credits, report the birth to the Tax Credit Office within one month.

You do not need to wait for child benefit to be awarded before getting child tax credit, as this may mean losing money.

The amount of child tax credit varies according to your circumstances and income, so not everyone gets the same amount. If you are on a low income, child tax credit is worth a lot more than child benefit and is the main source of support for your child. Extra amounts are payable if your child has a disability.

You must be aged at least 16 to qualify for child tax credit. If you are under 16, someone you live with (eg, your parent) can claim child tax credit for you and also for your baby.

You must normally be living with your child.

You may not count as being responsible for your child if s/he is in care and her/his maintenance or accommodation is paid for out of public funds. See Chapter 9 for more information.

Healthy Start vouchers and vitamins

Remember to notify Healthy Start once your baby is born in order to continue getting vouchers and vitamins. You get an extra voucher during your baby's first year.

If you did not qualify during pregnancy, you may now qualify, especially if you are now entitled to universal credit or child tax credit.

Sure Start maternity grant

If you did not qualify for a Sure Start maternity grant while you were pregnant, check whether you qualify now, especially if you are getting universal credit or child tax credit.

You must apply for a Sure Start maternity grant within six months of your baby's birth. Even if you have claimed and are waiting to hear about universal credit, you should still apply for the Sure Start maternity grant within six months of the birth.

Best Start in Scotland

Contact Social Security Scotland when your baby is born. If you are already getting Best Start foods, the amount is increased for a baby under one. If you did not qualify for Best Start foods or a Best Start grant during pregnancy, you may qualify if you are now entitled to universal credit. You must usually claim the Best Start grant pregnancy and baby payment within six months of the birth.

When your child is aged two, you may be entitled to the Best Start grant early learning payment. This is £250 per child aged two to three and six months. You can apply at any time from the second birthday until six months after the third birthday, as long as you meet the qualifying conditions when you apply.

When your child is able to start school, you can apply for the Best Start grant school age payment. This is £250 per child, payable from 1 June in the calendar year that s/he turns five, or if s/he was born in January or February, the calendar year in which s/he turns four – you must claim before the end of February in the following year. This ties in with when your child is able to start school, but it does not matter whether s/he has actually started school or not, for example if you have deferred her/his place.

You don't have to have received the pregnancy and baby payment in order to receive the early learning payment or school age payment.

Scottish child payment

Scottish child payment is being introduced for families living in Scotland, to top up 'means-tested benefits' by an extra £10 a week for each child under the age of six. Payments are due to begin in February 2021. It is expected that you will qualify if you are responsible for a child under the age of six, and you or your partner are getting any amount of:

• universal credit
• child tax credit or working tax credit
• income support
• income-based jobseeker's allowance
• income-related employment and support allowance
• pension credit

You can still get Scottish child payment if one of these benefits has been reduced to nil due to a sanction. You can still get Scottish child payment even if you are not getting an extra element for the child in these benefits due to the 'two-child limit'. You can get Scottish child payment if you are a 'kinship carer' and you are getting one of these benefits for yourself and the child lives with you.

It is expected that payments will end when your child turns six. However, the Scottish government plans to extend this to children under 16 by the end of 2022.

You will be able to apply at mygov.scot/benefits.

5. Are you a young parent?

If you are a young parent, you may have a choice about whether you are entitled to some support in your own right or whether someone else (usually your parent or guardian) claims for you.

If you are under 16, you can claim child benefit for your child in your own right. You could also be entitled to maternity allowance if you have been working – even a weekend or part-time job could be enough to qualify.

You cannot claim universal credit until you reach the age of 16.

If you are 16 or over and still in full-time 'non-advanced education' (such as at school or college doing a course below university degree level), you may be able to choose between claiming universal credit for yourself and allowing someone else to claim, or to continue claiming, universal credit or child tax credit for you. In this situation, there are a lot of things to consider, such as whether you want the financial independence of being responsible for your own money, and whether you would be better off – the amounts can work out very differently depending on your circumstances.

If you are a lone parent aged 16 or 17 and you claim universal credit, you do not have to look for work or have any other 'work-related requirements' in order to receive benefit.

If someone else is claiming universal credit or child tax credit for you and your baby, s/he can also claim a Sure Start maternity grant for your baby.

You are entitled to Healthy Start vouchers and vitamins (or Best Start foods in Scotland) while you are pregnant and under 18. You are also entitled if you are under 20 and someone else is claiming a qualifying benefit for you.

What CPAG says

Advice for young parents

- You do not have to give up your education or training.

- You do not have to give up work.

- Do not miss out on help.

- If you live with your parents, get advice on whether they should claim benefits for you, or whether you should make a claim yourself – the amount may be different.

- If you live on your own, you can claim benefits as a lone parent.

- If your partner lives with you (s/he does not have to be your baby's parent) and you are both aged at least 16, you count as a couple and her/his income may affect your benefits.

6. Are you adopting a child?

If you are adopting a child, the financial help to which you are entitled depends on whether the child has been placed with you before being adopted, or whether you have formally adopted her/ him.

Has a child been placed with you for adoption?

- You can qualify for a Sure Start maternity grant (in England and Wales) if you are adopting a child under 12 months, and you are getting a qualifying benefit. You must claim within six months of the date the child is placed with you for adoption, and before the child's first birthday. You cannot qualify if there is another child aged under 16 in your family.

- You can qualify for a Best Start grant pregnancy and baby payment (in Scotland) if a child under 12 months has been placed with you by an adoption agency, and you are getting a qualifying benefit. You must apply before the child's first birthday.

- You may be entitled to statutory adoption pay instead of statutory maternity pay. Statutory adoption pay is payable for 39 weeks, starting from (at the earliest) 14 days before the date you expect the child to be placed with you. If you are jointly adopting a child with your partner, either of you may be entitled to statutory adoption pay, but only one of you can claim it. If you get statutory adoption pay, your partner may be entitled to statutory paternity pay. You can decide to give up your statutory adoption pay and take statutory shared parental pay between you instead.

- You are entitled to child benefit under the normal rules.

- If you are already getting tax credits, you can usually get child tax credit for the child you will adopt as soon as s/he comes to live with you, unless the local authority is making payments to you under certain legal provisions. The 'two-child limit' does not apply, so you still get an amount for an adopted child even if you have two or more other children.

- You cannot get a 'child element' in your universal credit for a child placed with you while s/he is still being looked after by the local authority, unless you have parental responsibility for the child.

- Adoption allowances that you use to spend on the child do not affect your entitlement to benefits.

- Housing benefit and council tax reduction are not normally affected when a child is placed with you for adoption – you do not get additional benefit for the child but you are allowed one additional bedroom in the calculation of your rent (sometimes known as the 'bedroom tax').

- You can get Healthy Start vouchers and vitamins for a child aged under four who is placed with you for adoption if you get universal credit or child tax credit for her/him. In Scotland, you can get Best Start foods if a child has been placed with you by an adoption agency and you get a qualifying benefit.

Have you adopted a child?

- You can claim, or continue to claim, child benefit.

- Once the child is no longer looked after by the local authority and you are responsible for her/him, you can get a 'child element' in your universal credit.

- You can continue to get child tax credit.

- An adopted child is not affected by the 'two-child limit', so a child element is payable for her/him and does not reduce elements for any other children you have.

- Your housing benefit and council tax reduction include amounts for the child.

- You can qualify for Healthy Start vouchers and vitamins for an adopted child under the age of four (or in Scotland, Best Start foods for an adopted child under the age of three), provided you are getting a qualifying benefit.

Further information

For more information about the Healthy Start scheme, see healthystart.nhs.uk
Healthy Start Issuing Unit helpline: 0345 607 6823.

Sure Start maternity grant helpline: 0800 169 0140

For more information about Best Start in Scotland, see mygov.scot/best-start-grant-best-start-foods.
Social Security Scotland helpline: 0800 182 2222

Maternity Action provides free advice on rights at work, maternity pay and benefits to pregnant women, new mothers and fathers, trade unions, advisers and employers.
Maternity rights advice line: 0808 802 0029
maternityaction.org.uk

Working Families gives advice on employment rights for parents and on benefits for families.
Helpline: 0300 012 0312
advice@workingfamilies.org.uk
workingfamilies.org.uk

Family Lives provides information, advice, guidance and support on any aspect of parenting and family life.
Helpline: 0808 800 2222
familylives.org.uk

Gingerbread provides support and advice for single parents on anything from dealing with a break-up to moving into work and sorting out maintenance, benefit or tax credit issues.
Helpline: 0808 802 0925
gingerbread.org.uk

One Parent Families Scotland provides support and advice on anything from dealing with a break-up, to moving into work and sorting out maintenance, benefit or tax credit issues.
Helpline: 0808 801 0323
opfs.org.uk

Chapter 3
Child maintenance

This chapter covers:

1. What help is available?

2. How do you apply for child maintenance?

3. How much money do you get?

4. What should you do if your circumstances change?

5. Are you unhappy with the amount of maintenance you get?

6. Do you pay maintenance to someone?

What you need to know

- If you are the main carer of a child and her/his other parent lives elsewhere, you can get financial help from that person.

- You can choose to arrange this by yourself or use a government scheme. Some parents can use the courts.

- Child maintenance does not affect your benefits, so it can really help with the costs of bringing up children.

1. What help is available?

All parents are legally obliged to support their children financially until they are 16, sometimes until they are 20. If you are the main carer for your child and her/his other parent does not live with you, you may be able to get child maintenance – money the other parent pays you to help with the costs of your child. Child maintenance is often called 'child support'.

You can also get child maintenance if you are the main carer for someone else's child and her/his parents(s) live elsewhere. For example, if you are a grandparent or other relative who is the main carer of a child, you may be able to get child maintenance from both her/his parents.

You do not have to arrange or apply for child maintenance if you do not want to. It is up to you.

Getting child maintenance can make a big difference to your household budget. It does not affect any of your benefits. As long as it is money for your children, it is paid on top of all benefits to which you are entitled. You may also get maintenance for yourself. If this is the case, this *does* count as income and could affect your benefits.

2. How do you apply for child maintenance?

When can you get child maintenance?

If you have children who live with you, or mainly live with you, and one or both of their parents live elsewhere, you may be able to get child maintenance from the parent(s) to help support them. If your children have different parents, you can get maintenance from both/ all of them.

The children must be under 16, or under 20 and still in full-time, 'non-advanced education'. This means education at a school or college, studying for GCSEs, A levels, Scottish Highers and other courses which are below university level. A child in this situation is known as a 'qualifying child'.

> **EXAMPLE**
>
> **Getting maintenance**
>
> Tianna has three children living with her. Damon is 18 and doing an apprenticeship. Alex and Patrice are six. Tianna can get child maintenance for the twins, but not for Damon as he is not a qualifying child. The apprenticeship does not count as non-advanced education.

Do you want to apply?

You must decide whether you want to get child maintenance. There are lots of factors to consider, including whether the other parent sees the children and how much time they spend together. Remember, you do not have to ask for child maintenance – it is up to you – but your children are entitled to financial support from both parents.

If you are worried about the effect of child maintenance on the children's relationship with their other parent, it may help to discuss this. You can talk to one of the organisations that support separated parents.

What are your options?

If you decide you want child maintenance, the next step is to decide which option to choose.

• You can agree something with your child's other parent. This is known as a 'family-based arrangement'.

• You can apply to the Child Maintenance Service, which is a government agency. The child maintenance scheme run by the Child Maintenance Service is based on regulations.

• You can make an agreement with the other parent which becomes legally binding through the courts. This is often the option used by people who have been married to each other.

In the past, you may have received child maintenance under a previous government scheme through the Child Support Agency. Its cases are all now closed, but some people may still be owed arrears of child maintenance from cases under this previous scheme. The Child Support Agency may still be trying to get payment of these arrears for you.

If you have had a Child Support Agency case in the past, you still have the same choices as other parents. You can choose a family-based arrangement or you can apply to the Child Maintenance Service.

What is a family-based arrangement?

A family-based arrangement means that you and the other parent decide how much maintenance will be paid and when. If the other parent stops paying, you cannot take any enforcement action. Mediation can help you to decide on the terms of the arrangement and can be cheaper than legal advice.

The government has set up a service called Child Maintenance Options, to help parents understand child maintenance and which option will suit them best. You can use the child maintenance calculator provided by Child Maintenance Options to check how much the other parent would pay if you made an application to the Child Maintenance Service. Alternatively, you can work out an amount that reflects the costs of your children and how you want to share these costs. The Child Maintenance Options website has a form you can use to write down the details of your agreement with the other parent. However, it is important to understand that writing it down does not make it legally binding.

EXAMPLE

A family-based arrangement

Chris and Ian are separated. Their child Penny lives most of the time with Chris, but Ian helps to pick Penny up from school and also looks after her during the school holidays.

Chris and Ian come to an agreement based on the Child Maintenance Options calculator and are able to negotiate so that the amount reflects their different costs and income. Ian pays £60 a week in term time, but less in the school holidays.

The arrangement works well for Chris, but if Ian stopped paying or reduced the amount she would not be able to enforce it.

What is the Child Maintenance Service?

The Child Maintenance Service calculates child maintenance (also known as 'child support') for people who apply and who are eligible. It has replaced the Child Support Agency, which used to do this work.

You can apply to the Child Maintenance Service for it to work out how much child maintenance the other parent should pay, using rules set by the government. There is a £20 application fee, which you must pay. The fee is waived if you have experienced domestic violence or abuse, or if you are aged 18 or under. If this applies to you, tell the Child Maintenance Service straight away.

EXAMPLE

Child Maintenance Service 'collect and pay' fees

Ava's four children live with her. The Child Maintenance Service calculates that her former partner Joe, who is the father of all four children, should pay Ava £35 a week child maintenance. If direct pay is used, Joe pays £35 a week direct to Ava.

If the collect and pay service is used, Joe pays £42 a week (£35 + (20 per cent x £35)) to the Child Maintenance Service. The Child Maintenance Service deducts £1.40 (4 per cent x £35) from the child maintenance due to Ava, so she receives only £33.60 a week. The Child Maintenance Service keeps the balance of £8.40 a week.

The Child Maintenance Service usually prefers the other parent to pay the child maintenance to you directly. This is known as 'direct pay'. If you have experienced domestic violence or abuse, you should tell the Child Maintenance Service and it should explain how to make a direct pay agreement that will keep you safe. Alternatively, the Child Maintenance Service can collect the money from the other parent and then pay you. This is known as 'collect and pay'. You cannot choose this option unless the other parent agrees or there is a problem with payment. If the other parent does not pay you or fails to pay you the correct amount, tell the Child Maintenance Service and ask it to use collect and pay. However, using collect and pay means that the paying parent pays an extra 20 per cent and the money you receive is reduced by 4 per cent.

Box A
Pros and cons of child maintenance arrangements

Family-based	Child Maintenance Service
Can agree a higher amount.	Amount is set by the government's calculation, and there is a maximum amount even if the other parent is a very high earner.
Can adjust by agreement.	Changes in circumstances must be reported to the Child Maintenance Service, and only changes which affect the calculation are taken into account.
No fees.	Application fees.
Can arrange payment to suit.	Payment amounts are fixed. Collect and pay is not always possible, reduces the amount of your maintenance and costs the other parent.
Could avoid conflict.	Could create, or worsen, conflict with the other parent and could lead to disagreement about any shared care of the children.
Not possible if you cannot negotiate.	Does not require communication with the other parent.
Cannot be enforced.	Can be enforced according to set rules – but only if the Child Maintenance Service decides to take action.

Before using the Child Maintenance Service, you must talk to Child Maintenance Options, the organisation which explains child maintenance on behalf of the government. It is not possible to make an application without going through Child Maintenance Options first. Child Maintenance Options can talk through the advantages and disadvantages of family-based arrangements and more formal arrangements like the Child Maintenance Service or the courts, and explain the costs of using the Child Maintenance Service if these apply.

What about going to court?

It is possible to use the courts system to have a child maintenance agreement made formally binding. This is called a 'consent order' in England and Wales, and a 'minute of agreement' in Scotland. Mediation may help you to decide on the terms of the agreement, avoiding higher legal costs – but in Scotland, the agreement is usually written by your solicitor.

A binding agreement like this means that, if the other parent stops paying maintenance, you can go back to court to get the order enforced. However, after the order has been in force for at least a year, you (or the other parent) could also choose to make an application to the Child Maintenance Service. This means that, after the first year, it is harder to have this kind of binding agreement enforced.

Usually the courts are used when parents are divorcing and the order includes other issues – eg, payment of a mortgage. However, it is not necessary to use the courts and it can be a lot cheaper not to do so, if parents can agree.

Box B
Pros and cons of going to court

Advantages	Disadvantages
Can include other issues, such as housing costs.	May require legal advice, which usually has to be paid for.
Can be enforced through the court in the first year.	Involves fees and a formal court process.
	Changing the payments means applying to the court.
	Getting the order enforced can cost money and may be harder to do after the first year.
	Once you have a consent order or a minute of agreement, you cannot apply to the Child Maintenance Service for the next 12 months. After the first 12 months, the other parent can apply to the Child Maintenance Service – s/he may be likely to do this if the amount s/he would pay under the calculation is lower than the amount under the court order. This application then overrides the consent order or minute of agreement.

3. How much money do you get?

If you make an agreement with the other parent, the amount of child maintenance you get depends on what you agree. You can do this as part of a mediation process, or you may be able to have the conversation without using a mediator. You can use the calculator provided by Child Maintenance Options as a guide.

If you apply to the Child Maintenance Service, the amount of child maintenance is based on the circumstances of the other parent and the number of children.

The other parent's gross weekly income is used in the calculation. This is income before tax and national insurance are deducted. It includes her/his earnings, pension income and some other taxable income, but not interest on savings or rent from property. Only the other parent's income is taken into account. If s/he lives with a new partner, the partner's income is ignored.

There are different rates of maintenance.

Some parents do not have to pay anything. This is called the nil rate. The nil rate applies to very young parents (those for whom someone still receives child benefit, or those who are under 18 and get a means-tested benefit), prisoners, some people in care homes or independent hospitals, and some people who have a very low income.

If the other parent is on certain benefits or has an income of £100 a week or less, s/he pays a flat rate of £7 a week.

EXAMPLE

Reduced rate child maintenance

Mia has two children. Their father Tim does not live with them and only occasionally sees the family. Tim works variable hours at the minimum wage, but over the last few months his gross earnings have averaged £180 a week. Mia applies to the Child Maintenance Service and the reduced rate is used. Tim's weekly income is £80 above the £100 threshold. Twenty-five per cent of £80 = £20. This is added to £7. Tim must pay £27 a week.

A reduced rate of maintenance applies if the other parent's gross income is over £100 but under £200 a week. In this case, the other parent pays £7 a week plus a percentage of the amount of income s/he has over £100 a week:

- 17 per cent for one child
- 25 per cent for two children
- 31 per cent for three or more children

These percentages are reduced if the other parent has other children living with her/him. The amount of the reduction depends on the number of children.

EXAMPLE

Basic rate child maintenance

Pretesh and Joni are separated and have two children, aged 12 and eight. Joni has the main care of the children. Pretesh comes to see them once a week, but does not stay overnight. Pretesh has one younger child who lives with him and his new partner. Pretesh earns £650 a week gross.

Joni applies to the Child Maintenance Service and the basic rate is used.

Pretesh's income is first reduced by 11 per cent because he has one child living with him – giving £578.50.

Pretesh then pays 16 per cent of £578.50 = £92.56 a week.

The £92.56 is paid on top of any benefits Joni receives and can go directly to support the family.

Otherwise, a parent pays the basic rate of maintenance. This is worked out by first deducting an amount from the other parent's gross weekly income for any other children who are living with her/him:

- 11 per cent of gross income for one child
- 14 per cent of gross income for two children
- 16 per cent of gross income for three or more children

Once the deduction has been made, if the parent's remaining gross weekly income is £800 or less, s/he pays the following percentage of her/his income in maintenance:

- 12 per cent for one child
- 16 per cent for two children
- 19 per cent for three or more children

If the parent's remaining gross weekly income is over £800, s/he pays the relevant percentage above of the first £800 of her/his income in maintenance *plus* an additional percentage of any income over £800:

* 9 per cent for one child
* 12 per cent for two children
* 15 per cent for three or more children

EXAMPLE

Basic rate child maintenance

Consuela and Fred are separated with one child. Fred visits, but does not stay overnight. Fred earns £1,200 a week gross and has no other children.

Consuela applies to the Child Maintenance Service and the basic rate is used.

First, Fred's income up to £800 is looked at to calculate how much basic maintenance he must pay. Twelve per cent of £800 = £96. Next, his income above £800 is looked at to calculate how much additional maintenance he must pay. Fred has £400 excess income. Nine per cent of £400 = £36. So the total amount of maintenance he must pay is £96 plus £36 = £132 a week.

If the children a parent is paying child maintenance for have different other parents, the child maintenance due is split between those other parents. It is split in proportion to the number of children each of the other parents is looking after.

If some children of a relationship live with one parent and the other children live with the other parent, both parents may have to pay child maintenance. The payments are usually offset, so that only the parent who owes more actually pays anything.

Apportionment

Rhys has two children. Rosie lives with her mother Kate. Jack lives with his mother Kelly. Rhys is due to pay £39 a week child maintenance. As Kate and Kelly each look after one child, the child maintenance is split equally between them and they each receive £19.50 a week from Rhys.

Divided families

James and Amanda are separated. They have two children, Liam and Emma. Liam lives with James and Emma lives with Amanda. Both James and Amanda have to pay child maintenance for one child. Their gross weekly incomes are different. James is due to pay Amanda £54 a week for Emma. Amanda is due to pay James £24 a week for Liam. The payments due are offset, so James pays Amanda £30 a week (£54 – £24).

Does the other parent also look after the child?

If the other parent looks after the child overnight for at least one night a week (on average), this reduces the amount of child maintenance s/he must pay under the Child Maintenance Service calculation.

A parent who pays the basic or reduced rate of maintenance has this amount reduced by:

- one-seventh for 52 to 103 nights of care a year
- two-sevenths for 104 to 155 nights of care a year
- three-sevenths for 156 to 174 nights of care a year
- one-half for 175 or more nights of care a year

EXAMPLE

Shared care

Tim moves into a new flat and is able to have the children stay with him for two nights a week on a regular basis, which Mia is happy with.

The amount of child maintenance he must pay is reduced by two-sevenths of £27 = £7.71. He must now pay £19.29 a week.

If the day-to-day care of your child is shared absolutely equally between you and the other parent, there may be no child maintenance liability, even if the other parent earns more than you. You could still make a family-based arrangement.

4. What should you do if your circumstances change?

If your circumstances, or the other parent's circumstances, change, you may need to stop child maintenance or change the amount you get. For example, if a child no longer lives with you, your child maintenance could stop or the amount could go down. If the other parent gets a better paying job, the amount of your child maintenance could increase.

If you have a family-based arrangement, you should discuss the change with the other parent. You can still use the Child Maintenance Options calculator as a guide.

If you are using the Child Maintenance Service, tell it about the change, so that it can check the calculation.

If you have a court order, you will need to apply to the court to change the amount.

EXAMPLE

Change of circumstances

Priya's eldest son is 18 and leaves school in the summer. Because he is no longer in full-time non-advanced education, his father, Jon, does not need to pay child maintenance for him any longer. However, Jon's two other children are under 16 and still living with Priya.

Priya has a family-based arrangement and agrees that the child maintenance she gets will reduce. Even though her son continues to live with her, she cannot force Jon to pay maintenance for him, even if she was using the Child Maintenance Service or the courts.

5. Are you unhappy with the amount of maintenance you get?

If you are getting child maintenance under a family-based arrangement, but you are not happy with the amount, you could try to negotiate with the other parent. There might be specific expenses s/he could help with, such as school trips, or s/he may agree to pay more on a regular basis. Alternatively, you could consider using the Child Maintenance Service instead. Get advice to check whether the Child Maintenance Service calculation will result in your getting more money.

If you are using the Child Maintenance Service, but you think the calculation does not represent the other parent's actual income, you can ask for a 'variation'. A variation allows the calculation to be altered to take into account a different level of income. Variations can only be made in certain situations. For example, if you think the other parent has income which has not been taken into account in the calculation or has substantial assets, you can apply for a variation. Depending on the circumstances, it may help if you can provide the Child Maintenance Service with information.

What should you do if the other parent is not paying?

If the other parent is not paying, your options depend on the sort of child maintenance you have arranged.

If you have a family-based arrangement, you cannot force the other parent to pay. You may be able to negotiate. If you cannot find a way forward, you could consider making an application to the Child Maintenance Service.

If you are using the Child Maintenance Service, you can ask it to enforce payment. If you are using 'collect and pay', the Child Maintenance Service will know that payments have stopped. If the other parent pays you directly, tell the Child Maintenance Service that payment has stopped. Bear in mind that if you ask the Child Maintenance Service to collect the maintenance for you in the future, it will reduce the amount you receive, as well as costing the other parent more.

If you have a court order, you must apply to the court to enforce it.

6. Do you pay child maintenance to someone?

If you or your partner pay child maintenance to your child's other parent or main carer and you also have other children who live with you, or you provide some care for children who do not live with you full time, you should check that the amount you pay reflects these circumstances. You could use the Child Maintenance Service calculation to do this, even if there is no application to the Child Maintenance Service.

If the amount of maintenance you pay has been calculated by the Child Maintenance Service, this can only be changed (by applying for a 'variation') in limited circumstances – eg, if you pay for boarding school fees, or you have extra expenses because of a disabled child.

If you pay the flat rate, your weekly child maintenance and any 'collect and pay' fee can be deducted from your benefits by the Department for Work and Pensions and sent to the Child Maintenance Service. Deductions can also be made for arrears of child maintenance, but not at the same time as deductions for ongoing weekly child maintenance. Deductions mean that your benefit will be reduced before you get it.

Further information

CPAG's *Child Support Handbook* provides detailed information about the Child Maintenance Service scheme, including calculations and enforcement.

Child Maintenance Options provides information to help you compare the different ways you can set up a child maintenance arrangement: cmoptions.org.

The Child Maintenance Service is at childmaintenanceservice.direct.gov.uk/public.

In England and Wales, Gingerbread has lots of information about child maintenance on its website, and further support is available from its helpline: 0808 802 0925 or see gingerbread.org.uk.

In Scotland, One Parent Families Scotland has factsheets about child maintenance and also provides a helpline for lone parents: 0808 801 0323 or see opfs.org.uk.

Chapter 4
Childcare and school costs

This chapter covers:

1. What help is available?

2. Is your child entitled to free childcare?

3. Can you get help with your childcare costs?

4. What other help is there before your child goes to school?

5. What help can you get once your child starts school?

6. What happens to your benefits once your child reaches school-leaving age?

What you need to know

- Some help with childcare is free and available to all. Other help is available to working parents through universal credit or working tax credit.

- You may be able to get help with some school-related costs if you are on a low income. Your entitlement to help may change when your child reaches school-leaving age.

1. What help is available?

As your child gets older, there are some changes to the support available, including help for your child to participate in early education and childcare, such as going to pre-school, nursery or a childminder. Once your child starts school, there is also some support available to help her/him participate fully in school and continue in education. The support available is different in England, Scotland and Wales.

Box A

Financial help for childcare and education: checklist

- free education and childcare for two to four year olds
- help from your employer
- additional amounts in universal credit, working tax credit and housing benefit
- tax-free childcare scheme
- free nursery milk for under five year olds
- Healthy Start vouchers and vitamins for under four year olds in England and Wales
- Best Start and Scottish child payment in Scotland
- free school meals
- school clothing grants
- free transport to school

2. Is your child entitled to free childcare?

Some childcare and early education is available free of charge. Childcare providers must be registered. The rules vary between England, Scotland and Wales and depend on your child's age.

England

When your child reaches two years old, you may be entitled to 570 hours of free childcare a year. This works out as 15 hours a week over 38 weeks of the school year, which can be used flexibly.

You qualify for this if you or your partner get any of the following:

- universal credit
- income support
- income-based jobseeker's allowance
- income-related employment and support allowance
- child tax credit and/or working tax credit – your annual income must be under £16,190 before tax (unless you were getting working tax credit and it is less than four weeks since you stopped work)

- the 'guarantee credit' of pension credit
- asylum support

You also qualify if your child:

- is looked after by the local authority
- has a current statement of special educational needs or an education, health and care plan
- gets disability living allowance
- has left care under a special guardianship order, child arrangements order or adoption order

When a child is three years old, you are entitled to 570 hours of free childcare a year. This works out as 15 hours a week, which can be used flexibly. This is available to everyone – it does not depend on your income, work or benefits. The free childcare place starts from 1 January, 1 April or 1 September following your child's third birthday. Contact your local authority to claim your free childcare place.

Are you entitled to more hours?
If you are in paid work, you may be entitled to an additional 570 hours of free childcare if your child is three or four years old. This means you get 1,140 hours in total – around 30 hours a week, which can be used flexibly.

You and your partner must usually both be in work. You must expect to earn (on average) an amount equal to at least 16 hours at the national minimum wage rate for your age.

If you or your partner are on maternity, paternity or adoption leave, or you are unable to work because you are disabled or have caring responsibilities, you could still be eligible.

You cannot get this additional 30 hours of free childcare if either you or your partner expect to earn £100,000 or more a year.

You can find out more and apply online for 30 hours' free childcare in England at childcarechoices.gov.uk.

Wales

In some areas of Wales, under the Flying Start scheme, you may be entitled to free childcare for two and a half hours a day, five days a week for 39 weeks a year from the term after your child turns two, and at least 15 sessions during the school holidays. The Flying Start scheme is available to children under four years old who live in some areas in Wales. Contact your local authority to find out whether you live in a Flying Start area.

The childcare offer for Wales is 30 hours a week of free early education and childcare for working parents of three and four year olds for 48 weeks of the year. You qualify for this if you earn on average at least the minimum wage for 16 hours a week, and your individual gross earnings are less than £100,000 a year. Contact your local authority family information service to find out more about the support available in Wales.

Scotland

Once your child turns two, you may be entitled to 600 hours a year (about 16 hours a week in term time) of free early learning and childcare.

You qualify for this if you or your partner get any of the following:

- universal credit and your earnings are £610 or less in the month before you apply for the free childcare (if you have a partner, your joint earnings must be no more than £610 a month)
- income support
- income-based jobseeker's allowance
- income-related employment and support allowance
- incapacity benefit or severe disablement allowance
- pension credit
- child tax credit (but not working tax credit) and your income is less than £16,385 a year
- both child tax credit and working tax credit and your income is less than £7,320 a year
- asylum support

Your child can take up her/his funded childcare place from the term after her/his second birthday or from the term after you start receiving the qualifying benefit. Once your child becomes eligible and takes up her/his place, s/he remains entitled to a place even if your circumstances change – eg, if you no longer receive one of the above benefits.

If you are looking after a two year old child who is living with you under a 'kinship care' order or a parent guardianship order, or who is looked after by the local authority, you also qualify for the free early learning and childcare place.

All three and four year old children are entitled to 600 hours a year (around 16 hours a week during term time) of free early learning and childcare; you do not need to be getting a benefit. The Scottish government has committed to increasing this to 1,140 hours, but implementation of this has been delayed due to coronavirus.

3. Can you get help with your childcare costs?

Help with your childcare costs is available from the following sources.

- **Help from your employer.** Some employers provide their staff with childcare vouchers, direct payments to an approved childminder or nursery, or a workplace nursery.

- **Financial help through benefits.** Some social security benefits include help with the costs of childcare. These are universal credit, working tax credit and housing benefit. You must be entitled to the benefit in order to receive this.

- **'Tax-free childcare'.** This is a scheme in which the government tops up your contributions to a savings account specifically for paying for childcare.

Box B
What childcare counts?

In order to receive help with your childcare costs, the childcare must be provided by a registered childminder, nursery, school (eg, in an out-of-school-hours club) or other approved childcare provider. You cannot get help for childcare provided by a relative, unless s/he is registered and the care is provided outside your home.

You can check whether a childcare provider is approved at gov.uk/help-with-childcare-costs.

Can you get help from your employer?

Your employer is not legally obliged to provide you with help with childcare. However, some employers provide their staff with tax-free childcare vouchers of up to £55 a week, instead of the same amount of salary (known as 'salary sacrifice'). The voucher scheme has closed to new applicants but if you already get them, this arrangement can continue. You do not pay tax or national insurance on the amount of your salary provided by childcare vouchers.

Alternatively, your employer may arrange to pay your childcare costs directly to your childcare provider – eg, a nursery, crèche or after-school club. This is called 'directly contracted childcare' (or sometimes just 'direct payment'). You do not pay tax or national insurance on this help, within a set limit.

Some employers provide workplace nurseries. You do not have to pay tax or national insurance on this help.

Can you get help in your benefit?

Some benefits that are paid to people in work include specific amounts to help with the cost of childcare. These are universal credit, working tax credit and housing benefit. To qualify, you must be getting the benefit and you must be in paid work. In most cases, your partner must also be in paid work.

Universal credit

When working out your entitlement to universal credit, an extra amount called a 'childcare element' can be included to help you meet the cost of childcare. This can be for a child aged up to 16.

The amount of the childcare element is equivalent to 85 per cent of your childcare costs, up to a maximum of £646.35 a month for one child and £1,108.04 a month for two or more children.

EXAMPLE

Universal credit childcare element

Hala pays £1,250 a month for childcare for her three children. 85 per cent of this is £1,062.50. This is below the maximum payable of £1,108.04 a month for two or more children, so she can get reimbursed by a childcare element of £1,062.50 a month in her universal credit.

To get the childcare element included, you must be in paid work or have an offer of paid work that is due to start shortly. There are no minimum hours. If you are in a couple, your partner must also be in paid work, unless s/he has 'limited capability for work', is caring for a severely disabled person or is temporarily absent from home.

You should report the amount of childcare that you have paid in your online journal every month, so that your universal credit can be calculated correctly. Ask your childcare provider for receipts, as you may need to provide evidence or upload copies to your online journal. You can report the amount you have paid in the following month and they will be included, or up to 13 months after you have paid them if you are accepted as having a good reason for not reporting costs earlier.

You can get help with the childcare charges you have paid in the month before starting work, including a deposit, registration fee or advance charges. You can continue to get help with childcare costs in the month after stopping work.

If you have got into difficulties paying your childcare provider, the amount included in your universal credit can cover payment of arrears.

If you need to pay childcare costs so that you can start work, but cannot afford to pay until you receive the help from universal credit at the end of your monthly assessment period, you can ask your work coach to access the 'Flexible Support Fund', which can be used to pay your first month's childcare fees. Alternatively, you can ask for a 'budgeting advance' of universal credit. A budgeting advance is a discretionary payment, up to a maximum of £812, which can be payable straight away to help with work-related costs, and is recovered by deductions from your next payment of universal credit.

Working tax credit

If you already get tax credits, you can get help with childcare costs if you are working sufficient hours and start paying for registered childcare. When working out your entitlement to working tax credit, an extra amount called a 'childcare element' can be included to help you meet the cost of childcare. This can be for a child aged up to 15, or 16 if s/he is disabled.

The amount of the childcare element is equal to 70 per cent of your childcare costs, up to a maximum amount. This is £175 a week for one child or £300 a week for two or more children. So you can get up to £122.50 a week for one child, or £210 a week for two or more.

EXAMPLE

Working tax credit childcare element

Tracy pays £200 a week for a nursery place for her two children. This is below the maximum of £300 a week allowed for two children, so she can get a childcare element based on £200 a week. This is 70 per cent of £200 = £140 a week, or £7,280 a year.

If you are a lone parent, to qualify for the childcare element you must be working at least 16 hours a week.

If you are in couple, either you must both work at least 16 hours a week or one of you must work at least 16 hours a week and the other must be getting an incapacity or disability benefit (such as employment and support allowance or personal independence payment) or carer's allowance, or be in hospital or prison.

You must declare your average weekly childcare costs, or an estimate if you have just started paying for childcare. You must tell the Tax Credit Office if your childcare costs change by at least £10 a week for four weeks in a row. You can continue to get the amount for childcare costs for four weeks after you stop work, or stop paying for childcare. The Tax Credit Office may ask you to provide evidence at any time and may also check with your childcare provider.

Housing benefit
If you already get housing benefit some of your earnings can be ignored if you pay registered childcare costs. When working out your entitlement to housing benefit, some of your (and your partner's) earnings can be disregarded in order to help you with your childcare costs. This can be for a child aged up to 15, or 16 if s/he is disabled.

Up to £175 a week of your earnings can be disregarded for childcare costs for one child, and up to £300 a week for two or more.

If you are a lone parent, you must be working at least 16 hours a week.

If you are in couple, either you must both work at least 16 hours a week or one of you must work at least 16 hours a week and the other must be getting an incapacity or disability benefit (such as personal independence payment), or be in hospital or prison.

Tax-free childcare

If your income is too high for universal credit and you are not already getting tax credits, you may be able to get some help through tax-free childcare. The government contributes £2 for every £8 you pay into a savings account reserved for paying your registered childcare provider. Despite its name, the scheme does not have anything directly to do with tax. Some official information about the scheme, including a link for making an application, is available at gov.uk/get-tax-free-childcare.

The childcare must be for a child aged under 12, or 17 if s/he is disabled. You must be working and earning at least the rate of the national minimum wage appropriate for your age for a 16-hour week, and have a maximum income of £100,000 a year.

You can get up to £2,000 a year top-up for each child, or up to £4,000 for a disabled child.

What CPAG says

Tax-free childcare

Tax-free childcare may appear to have some advantages, but could leave you worse off if you are on a low income. You cannot get help through tax-free childcare if you are getting universal credit, child tax credit, working tax credit or childcare vouchers from your employer. If you apply for tax-free childcare, all your entitlement to tax credits is terminated and you cannot get any universal credit at the same time (not just the help with childcare costs). As universal credit and tax credits include amounts for basic needs as well as childcare, usually you will be much worse off on the tax-free childcare scheme.

4. What other help is there before your child goes to school?

Free nursery milk

If your child is under five years old and is in registered childcare or early education for two hours or more a day, s/he is entitled to about a third of a pint of milk each day. The milk can be any pasteurised cow's milk, including whole, semi-skimmed and organic. Fully-skimmed milk, goat's milk, soya milk, lactose-free milk, fluoridated milk, unpasteurised milk or milk with added flavours, colours, vitamins or other additives are not included. Babies under one are allowed fresh milk or specified brands of infant formula milk.

Healthy Start vouchers and vitamins

Do not forget that you continue to get vouchers for milk, fruit and vegetables and free vitamins from the Healthy Start scheme while your child is under four, whether or not s/he is in early education or childcare or receiving free nursery milk. Chapter 2 has more details on the scheme.

Best Start and Scottish child payment in Scotland

In Scotland, the Best Start foods payment card can continue until your child reaches three. You can apply for the Best Start grant early learning payment in Scotland from when your child is aged two to three and a half, and the school age payment when s/he is able to start school. You can apply for Scottish child payment at any time for a child under the age of six. Chapter 2 has more details on these schemes.

Free lunches in Scotland

In Scotland, children who qualify for free childcare or early education from age two are also entitled to a free lunch at their pre-school nursery.

5. What help can you get once your child starts school?

When your child starts school, you may find that there are unexpected costs connected to her/his education. As well as things like school uniforms and basic equipment, there may be other equipment, activities or trips that involve some additional spending. It is important that your child is able to participate fully in school, so make sure you are getting everything you are entitled to and not missing out on support.

What families say

School costs

'There's always something that you need to pay for... you're always getting a letter asking for something each month, you know, when it comes to school outings. And you don't want your child to miss out on that, so you're paying for it. Like there's always something you're having to pay for and not knowing that that's going to cover, you know, going to fit in your monthly bills as such. School uniform, it's all these little things...' *Mother*

Free school meals

Once your child starts school, s/he may be entitled to a free school meal. Some help is available to everyone (universal help); some is only for people on low incomes.

In England and Scotland, your child can get a free school lunch during her/his first three years of primary school. S/he can continue to get free school lunches in later years of primary school and in secondary school if you are on a low income.

In Wales, your child is entitled to a free breakfast if s/he attends a local authority primary school. S/he can only get a free school lunch if you are on a low income.

In England, Wales and Scotland, your child can get free school lunches if you have a low income. To qualify, you or your partner must get:

- universal credit
- income support
- income-based jobseeker's allowance
- income-related employment and support allowance
- child tax credit (but not working tax credit) and your annual income must be less than £16,190 in England and Wales, or £16,385 in Scotland
- in Scotland only, child tax credit and working tax credit and your annual income must be less than £7,330 (or you were getting

working tax credit and it is less than four weeks since you
stopped work)
- the 'guarantee credit' of pension credit (in England and Wales
  only)
- asylum support

If your child is between 16 and 18 and receiving any of the above
benefits in her/his own right, s/he can also get a free school lunch.

School clothing grant

You may qualify for a grant to help buy school uniforms and other
school clothing. Each local authority sets its own qualifying
conditions, but you usually qualify if you receive one of the benefits
that qualify you for free school meals. Some schools also provide
other help, such as uniform exchange schemes.

School transport

If you live more than a certain distance from your nearest suitable
school, or there is no safe walking route, local authorities must
provide your child with free transport to school if it is considered
necessary. Free school transport may also be provided if your child
has special educational needs or if you are on a low income – eg, if
you qualify for free school meals.

6. What happens to your benefits when your child reaches school-leaving age?

You can continue to get child benefit, child tax credit and amounts in
your universal credit for your child (the 'child element') until 1
September after her/his 16th birthday – even if s/he leaves school, or
is unable to attend school for any reason. Payments can also
continue if s/he stays on at school or if s/he goes to college,
provided the course s/he is doing is full time and 'non-advanced' or
if it is an approved training course. If this is the case, your child
benefit and child tax credit continue until her/his 20th birthday. The
child element in your universal credit continues to be included until 1
September after her/his 19th birthday.

Box C

What is full-time non-advanced education and approved training?

Full time means, on average, at least 12 hours a week during term time, including tuition, supervised study, exams and practical work, but not including meal breaks and unsupervised study. The course must normally be provided by a school or college. If your child is home-schooled, this can count if it began before the age of 16, or if it started after the age of 16 because of a disability.

Non-advanced courses include GCSEs, A levels and Scottish Highers, but not a university degree or a diploma.

Approved training. In England, training must count as 'appropriate full-time education', which means it is suitable for the young person's age, ability and aptitude, and to any special educational needs. In Wales, training must be a Traineeship or Foundation Apprenticeship. In Scotland, training must be provided under the Employability Fund, which is administered by Skills Development Scotland. A training course does not count as approved training if it is provided as part of a job.

You can still get child benefit and child tax credit if there is a reason why your child is temporarily unable to continue in education – for up to six months for some reasons, or indefinitely if it is due to an illness or disability.

You can continue to claim child benefit and child tax credit for a 16/17 year old who has left full-time non-advanced education or approved training, provided s/he has registered for work or training with the careers service. This period can continue for up to 20 weeks and you must report this within three months of the date s/he left education.

You cannot continue to claim in this period if s/he starts work for 24 hours or more a week.

You can continue to get child benefit, child tax credit and universal credit for a young person aged 19, but s/he must have started, enrolled, or been accepted on the course before turning 19. You can only get an amount for her/him in your universal credit until 1 September after her/his 19th birthday.

Make sure you tell the relevant office that deals with your child benefit, universal credit or child tax credit if your child is staying on in full-time non-advanced education or approved training after school-leaving age. Contact each office separately as you cannot rely on them sharing information. You should tell them each August/ September whether your child is continuing in education, and if s/he changes courses at any time during the year.

You should also report if your child is not living with you for any reason. Even if your child is living with you and continuing in full-time non-advanced education, there are some situations in which you cannot continue to claim child benefit, universal credit or child tax credit for her/him.

You cannot claim benefit for a young person if s/he is married or living with her/his partner as a couple and her/his partner is not in full-time non-advanced education or approved training. This is the case, even if they are both living with you.

You cannot claim for a young person if s/he claims universal credit, jobseeker's allowance, or employment and support allowance in her/his own right. Sometimes, you may be able to choose whether to continue claiming child benefit, universal credit or child tax credit for your child once s/he has reached school-leaving age, or whether s/he would be better off claiming universal credit in her/his own right.

What CPAG says

Universal credit for 19 year olds

CPAG thinks it is unfair that some 19 year olds in full-time non-advanced education cannot be included in their parents' universal credit claim, while they are also prevented from claiming universal credit in their own right. We are challenging these rules through legal action and campaigning. For more information, see cpag.org.uk/welfare-rights/resources/test-case/universal-credit-uc-19-year-olds-full-time-non-advanced-education.

Is there any other help for young people in education?

If your child is between 16 and 19 and continuing in full-time 'non-advanced education' in Scotland or Wales, s/he may be able to claim an education maintenance allowance, depending on your household income. The education maintenance allowance is payable at £30 a week.

In England, s/he may be able to get help with her/his studies from the '16 to 19 Bursary Fund', depending on the circumstances. In some situations, a vulnerable student bursary is payable at up to £1,200 a year if you are unable to support her/him or if s/he has a disability.

Discretionary bursaries may also be available from schools and colleges in England, Scotland and Wales.

If your child has moved on to full-time advanced education (university degree level), s/he will usually have to rely on student loans and any other discretionary grants available. See CPAG's *Student Support and Benefits Handbook* and *Benefits for Students in Scotland Handbook* for more information about when other help may be available.

Further information

More information on government support with childcare in England, Wales and Scotland is at childcarechoices.gov.uk.

For more information on childcare in Scotland, contact your local authority Family Information Service or see families.scot.

Find your local family information service in Wales at gov.wales/find-your-local-family-information-service.

For an official calculator to help work out childcare costs you can claim in working tax credit, see gov.uk/childcare-costs-for-tax-credits.

Coram Family and Childcare Trust:
020 7239 7535, email info@familyandchildcaretrust.org or see familyandchildcaretrust.org.

Chapter 5
Being out of work or in low-paid work

This chapter covers:

1. What help is available?

2. Are you looking after a young child?

3. Are you looking for work?

4. Are you in paid work?

5. What are your responsibilities?

6. Are you unable to work because you are sick or disabled?

What you need to know

- Benefits are available to help with your basic needs in a number of situations, including if you are looking for work, if you are in work on a low income, or if you are unable to work because you are ill or have a disability. Some depend on how much money you have coming in; some depend on your national insurance contribution record.

- In most cases, in order to get benefit, you must meet certain responsibilities related to work, such as attending interviews with the Department for Work and Pensions and undergoing retraining in order to increase your chances of finding a job.

- Benefits paid to you in work have rules about the amount of work you must be doing. Benefits for being unable to work because of illness or disability involve an official assessment of your capability for work.

1. What help is available?

If you are not in paid work, or if you are but your income is low, you may be able to claim social security benefits to help you meet your family's basic needs. You may be in one of the following situations:

- You may not be working because you are at home looking after your new baby or young children.

- You may have lost your job and are currently looking for work.

- You may be working, either part time or full time, but your earnings are insufficient to cover your costs.

- You may have a health condition or disability which means you cannot work, or you may be off work because you are ill.

If you are in one of the above situations, you may be able to claim universal credit, jobseeker's allowance or employment and support allowance to help top up your income or to compensate you for your loss of earnings. In order to get benefit, you must meet certain rules related to work. These are outlined in this chapter.

If you pay rent and your income is low, you may have a 'housing costs element' included in your universal credit. If you are on a low income, you may also get help with paying your council tax (council tax reduction). Chapter 6 has more information about the help you can get with your housing costs.

Do not forget you can also claim child benefit. There is more about this in Chapter 2.

> Box A
> **Financial help while you are out of work or in low-paid work: checklist**
> - universal credit
> - jobseeker's allowance
> - working tax credit (if you already get child tax credit)
> - statutory sick pay
> - industrial injuries benefits
> - employment and support allowance

2. Are you looking after a young child?

You do not have to look for work while you are responsible for a baby or a child under the age of three, but you can if you want to.

If you claim universal credit, you do not have to look for work. You can get universal credit if you are a lone parent or part of a couple. If you are part of a couple on universal credit, you and your partner should decide between you who you want to nominate as the responsible carer for your child(ren). This can only be changed once in the following 12 months or if there has been a change in your circumstances, such as one of you has stopped or started work. The following rules apply if you get universal credit.

- While your baby is under the age of one, you do not have any 'work-related requirements'.

- While your child is aged one, you are required to attend 'work-focused interviews' to discuss your future employability options. These are usually every six months, but may be more frequently. You can bring your child with you to the interview or request a payment for childcare costs, if this is not suitable. You should participate in the interviews but you do not need to agree to any follow-up action. Your universal credit may be sanctioned if you fail to attend the interview without a good reason.

- While your child is aged two, you are required to attend 'work-focused interviews' and undertake some activity to prepare for work, such as preparing a CV or attending skills training. If you need help with childcare costs to participate, ask your work coach. Your universal credit may be sanctioned if you refuse to undertake activity without a good reason. You do not have to look for work yet.

- When your child turns three, you are expected to look for work. It does not have to be full-time work. You need to agree to be available for some work, depending on suitable childcare being available. Your universal credit may be sanctioned if you refuse to look for work or take up a job without good reason.

If you claim jobseeker's allowance, you must look for work as agreed, whatever the age of your child.

3. Are you looking for work?

You usually have to look for work if you are a lone parent with a child aged three or over. You usually have to look for work if you are part of a couple and your partner is the lead carer for a child under three. Both you and your partner usually have to look for work when your youngest child reaches the age of three. If you are looking for work, the key benefits for meeting your and your family's basic needs are jobseeker's allowance and universal credit.

If you have worked in the past and paid enough national insurance contributions, you may be able to get jobseeker's allowance. This is only paid for a maximum of 182 days. Otherwise, you may be able to get universal credit.

You can be paid jobseeker's allowance at the same time as universal credit.

To get jobseeker's allowance or universal credit while looking for work, you must accept a 'claimant commitment' and fulfil certain responsibilities related to work.

You may also be able to get jobseeker's allowance if you are doing some part-time work. You can also get universal credit while you are working – there are no limits on the amount of work you can do.

4. Are you in paid work?

If you are in paid work, but your income is low, you may be able to claim benefit to top up your earnings.

If you already get child tax credit and start working sufficient hours, you can start to get working tax credit. This is being replaced by universal credit, so if you are not already getting child tax credit, you cannot make a new claim for working tax credit and must claim universal credit instead. Chapter 11 explains when you cannot claim universal credit.

If you are not working, or only working a few hours a week, you may be able to get jobseeker's allowance, depending on your national insurance record, and/or universal credit to help top up your income.

In-work poverty

'Managing, aye, I would say we are because it does, we've just not got money to do anything though or... buy anything, I suppose... I've got used to that... my mortgage is paid and all my bills are paid and then I've got food. That's, that's it.' *Parent of a disabled child*

'I have a zero-hour contract as a carer for an elderly lady. When my client went into hospital for a fortnight the company I work for didn't give me any other work. I was forced to take a week's annual leave to limit the loss of wages to one week instead of two.' *Lone parent*

'[Childcare costs £300 a month] which is annoying because I'm obviously only earning £600. So it's that way of you're literally, half of it's going straight away to childcare.' *Parent*

Jobseeker's allowance

What are the rules about work?

Jobseeker's allowance is a benefit based on national insurance contributions for people who are unemployed, but you can also be entitled while doing some part-time work. It is sometimes known as 'new-style' or 'contribution-based' jobseeker's allowance.

You must either be unemployed or working less than 16 hours a week. If you have a partner, it does not matter how much work s/he does.

To get jobseeker's allowance, even if you are working, you must accept a 'claimant commitment' in which you agree to do certain things in return for receiving benefit (known as your 'work-related requirements').

How are your earnings assessed?

The amount of jobseeker's allowance you get is reduced by certain types of income.

Your earnings are assessed on a weekly basis after £5 a week is disregarded.

Your 'net' earnings are taken into account. Your 'net' earnings are your earnings after deductions for income tax, class 1 national insurance contributions and half of any contribution you make towards a personal or occupational pension scheme. The amount of any personal or occupational pension over £50 a week is also taken into account.

Universal credit

What are the rules about work?

Universal credit is a benefit for people on a low income who are in paid work, as well as for people who are out of work. There are no rules about the amount of work you can or must do – you can claim universal credit even if you only work a few hours each week. However, to get universal credit, even if you are working, you must accept a 'claimant commitment' in which you agree to do certain things in return for receiving benefit (known as your 'work-related requirements').

If you only work a few hours each week and your earnings are low, the Department for Work and Pensions may expect you to be available for more work. This could be working more hours in your current job or working more hours (or earning more) in another job. However, once your earnings reach a certain level, you no longer need to be available for more work or to look for more work. The amount of this threshold is equivalent to the national minimum wage for someone of your age for a 35-hour week. If you have a child you may have a lower threshold.

If your earnings are below the threshold but are still below a certain level (£343 a month if you are single or £549 a month if you in a couple), you do not have to look for more work unless you are notified that you are part of the in-work conditionality pilot. You may still be required to attend work-focused interviews or take action to help you obtain more work or better paid work.

How are your earnings assessed?

The amount of universal credit you get depends on your income, so your earnings are taken into account, together with any other income you have that affects your entitlement – eg, certain benefits, including contributory employment and support allowance and carer's allowance, and income from a pension.

Your earnings include your basic wages, as well as any overtime, holiday pay and sick pay. They also include payments from your employer – eg, statutory sick pay or contractual sick pay, statutory maternity pay and statutory paternity pay.

Your earnings are assessed on a monthly basis. If you are employed, you need to check the amount of your earnings as shown on your online journal each month, which is automatically obtained from your employer when you are paid – this is called 'real-time information'. If you are self-employed, you must report your earnings every month.

Your net earnings are used – ie, after deductions for income tax, class 1 national insurance contributions and any contribution you make towards a personal or occupational pension scheme.

If you are self-employed, your gross monthly profit is used. This is worked out by deducting certain permitted expenses from your receipts. These can include things like rent, wages and insurance, purchase of equipment and stock, and VAT. If you have been self-employed and claiming universal credit for over a year, and your earnings are low, your universal credit may be based on higher earnings than you actually have. This amount is called the 'minimum income floor' and is usually set at the level of the national minimum wage for someone of your age for a 35-hour week.

People with children can earn up to a certain level without losing any universal credit. This is called a 'work allowance'. This is £292 a month if your universal credit includes housing costs, or £512 a month if it does not. If your (and your partner's combined) earnings are less than the work allowance, they are all disregarded. If they are more than the work allowance, your universal credit is reduced by 63 per cent of the amount above the work allowance.

> **EXAMPLE**
>
> **Assessing earnings for universal credit**
>
> Anne is a lone parent with a child aged six. Her universal credit includes an amount to help with her rent. She has a part-time job, earning £400 a month. Anne gets a work allowance of £292 a month when her universal credit is calculated. Anne's earnings exceed her work allowance by £108 (£400 – £292). So the amount of Anne's earnings taken into account as income for universal credit is 63 per cent of £108 = £68.04.

Working tax credit

What are the rules about work?

It is not usually possible to make a new claim for tax credits, but if you already get child tax credit, you can start to get working tax credit. To get working tax credit, you or your partner must normally work a minimum number of hours a week. The number depends on your age and circumstances.

It is the hours you normally work that count. So you can continue to qualify while you are on annual leave, or while you are getting statutory maternity or paternity pay, maternity allowance, statutory sick pay or employment and support allowance.

You can be employed or self-employed, or a mixture of the two. If you are self-employed, the work you do must be with a view to making a profit, and must be 'commercial, regular and organised'.

How many hours do you need to work?

Your circumstances	The number of hours you must work
You are under 25 years old, and either you have a child or a disability.	At least 16 hours a week.
You are aged 25 to 59.	At least 30 hours a week.
You are aged 60 or over.	At least 16 hours a week.
You have a disability.	At least 16 hours a week.
You are a lone parent.	At least 16 hours a week.
You are in a couple and have at least one child.	Usually at least 24 hours a week between you, with one of you working at least 16 hours a week. If you work less than 24 hours between you, you can still qualify if you work at least 16 hours a week and you are disabled or you are at least 60 years old, or if your partner gets a sickness or disability benefit or carer's allowance, or if s/he is in hospital or prison.

How are your earnings assessed?

The amount of working tax credit you get depends on your income, so your earnings are taken into account, together with any other income you have that affects your entitlement – eg, a taxable social security benefit, such as contribution-based jobseeker's allowance, and pension income. Usually, your initial award of working tax credit is based on what your income was in the previous tax year (April to April). Your earnings are then assessed on a monthly basis.

Your earnings include your basic wages, as well as any overtime, holiday pay and sick pay. The first £100 a week from statutory payments (such as statutory maternity pay and statutory paternity pay) is ignored.

Your gross pay is assessed, so it is the amount of your pay before deductions for income tax and national insurance contributions that is taken into account. However, any contributions you make to a personal or occupational pension are deducted and are not taken into account.

If you are self-employed, it is your taxable profits that are taken into account. When you claim working tax credit, you should declare the amount you included on your tax return for the last complete year. If you do not have this, you should estimate your profit. If you made a loss, your profit is 'zero'.

5. What are your responsibilities?

Most people must satisfy certain work-related responsibilities in order to get jobseeker's allowance and universal credit. The requirements that apply to you depend on your circumstances. You can negotiate about these with your 'work coach' or personal adviser at the job centre. If s/he agrees, you can, for instance, place limitations on the work you are looking for – eg, the type of work, its location, the number of hours and the rate of pay.

If you do not carry out your requirements, you may be 'sanctioned' and your benefit reduced. The sanctions can be severe, so you should always try to avoid one if you can.

What families say

Sanctions

'A lone parent with four children had a major loss of income over Christmas and had to attend a food bank because she was sanctioned for failing to attend an appointment when one of her children was rushed to hospital. The sanction was eventually lifted because the client had a good reason for missing the appointment, but it took two months to sort out.' *Community welfare rights adviser*

A sanction should not be applied if you have a good reason for your actions. If you are given a sanction, you can challenge it. Chapter 10 has more information on this.

What CPAG says

Avoiding a sanction

- If you cannot attend or you miss a work-focused interview, contact your work coach or personal adviser as soon as possible to explain why.

- Does your claimant commitment take into account any difficulties you have in looking for work? Make sure your work coach or personal adviser is aware of these and ask that they be taken into account.

- If you are finding it hard to carry out all the responsibilities in your claimant commitment, ask for it to be reviewed.

- If your circumstances change, tell your work coach or personal adviser straight away; your claimant commitment may also need to be changed.

- Keep a written record of everything you do to look for, or prepare for, work.

- If you do not think that a work placement or course is suitable for you, let your work coach or personal adviser know and ask not to take part in it.

- Try to stick to your claimant commitment, but if you have a good reason for not keeping to it (eg, because you have been ill), let your work coach or personal adviser know as soon as possible.

Accepting a claimant commitment

For jobseeker's allowance and universal credit, you must accept a 'claimant commitment'. This is a written record of what you must do in return for your benefit (your 'responsibilities'). If you do not accept a claimant commitment, you are not entitled to benefit, unless there are exceptional circumstances – eg, if you cannot act for yourself or you have a domestic emergency.

Box B
Your claimant commitment

- Your claimant commitment is drawn up with your work coach or personal adviser at the job centre. It can be completed online, by phone or in person.

- The commitment is a record of the responsibilities you must fulfil in order to get benefit – eg, what you must do to look for work and what your pattern of availability for work is. It also records how you will be sanctioned and your benefit reduced if you do not meet your responsibilities.

- Make sure you tell your work coach or personal adviser about any problems you have with looking for work and discuss what limitations you can be allowed.

- If you are unhappy with your claimant commitment, you can ask for it to be reviewed at any time. However, because you must accept a claimant commitment in order to get benefit, it is best to accept it first and then ask for it to be reviewed at a later date.

What are the work-related requirements for universal credit?

- **Attending work-focused interviews**. These are interviews, usually at the job centre, about your work prospects, and any training, education and rehabilitation that might help you.

- **Work preparation**. This is particular action that you may be required to carry out to be better prepared for work, such as attending a skills presentation or participating in an employment programme or work placement.

- **Work search**. This means taking all 'reasonable action' to look for work, regardless of the type of work or salary. You are usually expected to spend 35 hours a week looking for work. If you are caring for a child (or if you have a disability or are caring for someone with a disability), this can be less. You are usually expected to look for work in locations up to 90 minutes travel time from your home.

- **Work availability.** You must be able and willing to take up paid work (including more work or better paid work) immediately. This requirement can be eased if you are doing voluntary work and need longer notice, if you have caring responsibilities that require you to be given more time, or if you are already working and must give your employer notice that you are leaving the job. You must also be willing and able to attend a job interview immediately. You are usually expected to be available for work of at least 35 hours a week, unless you have caring responsibilities (including for a child aged under 16) or a disability.

Some people must meet all the 'work-related requirements'. You have fewer requirements placed on you if you have a child, but the requirements increase as your child reaches her/his first, second and third birthdays.

If you are in a couple, only one of you can have fewer requirements placed on you because you have a child. This is the partner who is the child's 'main carer'. You count as the child's main carer if you and your partner have nominated you.

If your youngest child is school age but under 13 years old, you only have to look for and be available for work during her/his normal school hours (including travelling time to and from school). You do not have to accept a job which would mean having to leave her/him on her/his own after school.

If your child is under 16, you do not have to accept a job which would mean having to leave her/him on her/his own during school holidays, if there is no one else to look after her/him.

Which work-related requirements apply?

People with children	
You are pregnant and there are 11 weeks or less before your baby is due, or you had a baby not more than 15 weeks ago.	No requirements.
You have a child under one year old, or you have adopted a child within the previous 12 months.	No requirements.
Your youngest child is one year old.	Work-focused interviews only.
Your youngest child is two years old.	Work-focused interviews and work preparation only.
Your youngest child is at least three years old.	Work-focused interviews, work preparation, work search and work availability.
You are a foster parent of a child under one year old.	No requirements.
You are a foster parent of a child aged between one to 16 years old.	Work-focused interviews only, if the child has care needs which make it unreasonable to expect you to do more.
You have experienced domestic violence.	No requirements for 13 weeks from when you notify the Department for Work and Pensions.

EXAMPLE

Universal credit work-related requirements

Ghita and Sanjay are not working and have a baby, Kapil. They claim universal credit. Ghita is Kapil's main carer and does not need to look for work, be available for work or attend interviews about work. When Kapil reaches one, Ghita may have to attend work-focused interviews.

Sanjay must look for work and be available for work and job interviews.

Which work-related requirements apply?

Other situations	
You have experienced domestic violence.	No requirements for 13 weeks from when you notify and no work search or availability requirements for a further 13 weeks if you have a child. You could be required to attend work-focused interviews or prepare for work after the first 13 weeks.
You are caring for a severely disabled person and you get carer's allowance, or you would get carer's allowance if you applied for it but for the fact that your earnings are higher than allowed.	No requirements.
You have a severe health condition or disability and have 'limited capability for work-related activity'.	No requirements.
You have a significant health condition or disability and have 'limited capability for work'.	Work-focused interviews and work preparation only.
You are working and your earnings are at least the level of a set earnings threshold.	No requirements.
You are working and you are earning at least a set amount (currently £338 a month if you are single or £541 a month if you are in a couple).	Work-focused interviews and work preparation only.
You are working and your partner or child has died within the last six months, or you are looking after a child and a death, violence or abuse has significantly disrupted your life in the last two years.	Work-focused interviews and work preparation only.

What are the jobseeking conditions for jobseeker's allowance?

Being available for work. You must usually be willing and able to take up work immediately, at any time, and to take a job of at least 40 hours a week (although you must also be prepared to work part time). You can be allowed more time if you are doing voluntary work (or providing some other service), if you have caring responsibilities, or if you are working part time and must give your employer notice that you are leaving your job.

If you are a lone parent with a child under 13 years old, you can restrict your availability to your child's usual school hours.

If you have a child under 16 years old, or are looking after someone with a disability or someone over 'pension age', you can be available for less than 40 hours' work a week, provided you are available to work at least 16 hours and you have a reasonable chance of getting work.

You are treated as being available for work in some situations. These include if your child is under 16 and it is unreasonable for you to make other arrangements during the school holidays, if there is a domestic emergency (eg, if one of your children is ill), or if you have experienced domestic violence and you have told the Department for Work and Pensions of this within the last four weeks.

Actively seeking work. You are usually expected to take at least three 'steps' each week to ensure you have the best prospects of getting work. Keep a record of what you have done. 'Steps' can include:

- applying for jobs
- seeking information about jobs
- registering with an employment agency
- preparing your CV
- making enquiries about jobs via the internet or email

You are treated as actively seeking work in some situations. These include if there is a domestic emergency (eg, if one of your children is ill), or if you have experienced domestic violence and you have reported this within the last four weeks.

6. Are you unable to work because you are sick or disabled?

If you are unable to work because you are sick or you have a long-term health condition or disability, you may be able to get benefit to help meet your basic needs.

Are you employed?

If you are employed but are incapable of doing your job because you are sick or you have a long-term health condition or disability, you may be able to get statutory sick pay from your employer. To qualify, you must have been earning enough to pay national insurance contributions. You cannot get statutory sick pay if you are entitled to statutory maternity pay or maternity allowance, or if you are self-employed.

Statutory sick pay is paid by your employer for a maximum of 28 weeks.

You may also be entitled to contractual sick pay from your employer. This depends on the terms of your contract. If you are entitled to contractual sick pay, your employer can deduct your statutory sick pay from your contractual sick pay.

If you are on a low income, your statutory sick pay (and contractual sick pay) can be topped up by universal credit.

If you are employed and disabled as a result of an accident at work or a disease caused by your job, you may be entitled to industrial injuries benefits. This does not apply if you are self-employed. To be entitled, you must have been injured in an industrial accident or have a prescribed industrial disease, and be assessed as being sufficiently disabled.

What if you do not get statutory sick pay?

If you are not entitled to statutory sick pay (including because you are not employed) or if you have received your full 28 weeks' entitlement and are still unable to work, you may be able to get employment and support allowance and/or universal credit. If you have worked in the past and paid enough national insurance contributions, you may be able to get employment and support allowance. This is sometimes known as 'new-style' or 'contributory' employment and support allowance.

If you have received your full entitlement to statutory sick pay, your employer should give you Form SSP1 to support your claim. You can get employment and support allowance even if you are still employed, but not if you have returned to work of 16 hours or more a week, or are earning more than £140 a week. If you work less than 16 hours and do not earn more than £140 a week, you can still get employment and support allowance in full. Employment and support allowance is reduced by 50 per cent of a private or occupational pension over £85 a week.

How is your ability to work assessed?

In order to get employment and support allowance, or universal credit on the basis of being too ill to work, you must have what is known as 'limited capability for work'.

You must first provide a medical certificate from your doctor. You will then usually have to have a 'work capability assessment'. This means that you must complete a questionnaire about your health and attend a medical examination. If you fail to return the questionnaire or miss the medical without a good reason, you are automatically treated as being fit for work.

Information from your doctor, the questionnaire and the medical examination is used to decide whether you score sufficient points to count as having limited capability for work. Some people, including people who have a terminal illness or who are receiving chemotherapy or radiotherapy for cancer, automatically pass the assessment.

In exceptional circumstances, you can be treated as having limited capability for work even though you would not otherwise do so. The most common of these situations is where there would be a substantial risk to your health (or to someone else's health) if you had to work, look for work or (if your condition is severe) undertake 'work-related activity'.

You are automatically treated as having limited capability for work if you are pregnant and there is a serious risk to your health or to your baby's health if you do not refrain from work.

You are automatically treated as having limited capability for work for employment and support allowance if you are pregnant and entitled to maternity allowance, if you are within six weeks of the expected date of the birth or you are within 14 days of having given birth.

For employment and support allowance, if you are waiting for an assessment to be carried out, you can be treated as having limited capability for work, and so get benefit while your medical examination is being arranged, provided you have submitted a medical certificate. However, if you are reclaiming after having already failed the assessment and your health condition has not changed or significantly deteriorated, this does not apply.

For universal credit, you are not treated as having limited capability for work while you are waiting for an assessment to be carried out. You can still get universal credit while you are waiting to be assessed, but you may be required to look for work. However, your 'work coach' has the discretion to waive this requirement in this situation, in particular if you have submitted a medical certificate and s/he considers it is unreasonable to expect you to look for work.

What are your work-related requirements?

Even though you have 'limited capability for work', in order to get your full entitlement of employment and support allowance you must still attend 'work-focused interviews' and undertake 'work-related activity', such as preparing a CV or basic skills training. You cannot be required to apply for a job or do any work, but you can agree to do work experience or voluntary work.

To get universal credit, you must still accept a 'claimant commitment' and to get your full entitlement, you must attend work-focused interviews and prepare for work. This is activity intended to make it more likely that you will return to work. The requirements must be reasonable and take all your circumstances into account.

However, as well as assessing your ability to work, the 'work capability assessment' also looks at whether you have what the law calls 'limited capability for work-related activity'. This is whether you are so ill or disabled that you cannot be expected to attend work-focused interviews, undertake work-related activity or prepare for work.

Your responsibilities may also be affected by your other circumstances, including if you have a young child. You do not have any work-related responsibilities if you are a lone parent with a child under one year old. For employment and support allowance, you continue not to have any work-related responsibilities while your youngest child is aged under three. For universal credit and employment and support allowance, your work-related responsibilities start to increase when your youngest child turns one.

If you get carer's allowance for looking after a disabled person, you do not have any work-related responsibilities.

If you fail to take part in an interview or refuse to undertake work-related activity without a good reason, you may be 'sanctioned'. This means the amount of your employment and support allowance or universal credit is reduced until you comply. 'Good reason' is not defined, but all your circumstances, including your illness, disability, caring responsibilities, language and transport problems, should be taken into account. If you have been sanctioned, you can challenge this. See Chapter 10 for more information.

Further information

More information about universal credit, sanctions and conditionality is available at AskCPAG.org.uk.

Full details about limited capability for work and the work capability assessment is in CPAG's *Welfare Benefits and Tax Credits Handbook*.

Chapter 6
Housing costs

This chapter covers:

1. What help is available?

2. Do you pay rent?

3. Are you paying a mortgage?

4. Can you get a discretionary housing payment?

5. Can you get help with your council tax?

6. Can you get help with fuel costs?

What you need to know

- If you are on a low income, you can get help with your rent through universal credit or, sometimes, housing benefit.

- You may get a loan to help with your mortgage if you get universal credit and some other benefits.

- You may be able to get council tax reduction to help with your council tax, or, in some cases, a discount on your council tax bill.

- You may be eligible for a winter fuel payment or other help with your fuel costs.

1. What help is available?

If you have a low income you may be able to get help with your rent, mortgage payments, council tax and fuel costs. This chapter explains what help is available.

Box A
Financial help for housing costs: checklist
- universal credit
- housing benefit
- discretionary housing payments
- council tax reduction
- winter fuel payment

2. Do you pay rent?

If you are on a low income, you may be able to get universal credit or housing benefit to help with paying your rent. You can get help whether you are in or out of work. It does not matter who your landlord is – you could be a council or housing association tenant, or you might have a private landlord. You can get help with your rent and certain service charges, such as some warden and caretaker services, communal lifts and entry phones.

You can get help with the rent on the home in which you normally live. In some limited situations, you can get help with the rent on two properties – eg, if you have had to move because of a fear of domestic violence.

Housing benefit for people who are under pension age is being replaced by universal credit. If you come under the universal credit system, you cannot make a new claim for housing benefit, and must claim universal credit instead. There are exceptions for people who live in certain types of accommodation, such as a domestic violence refuge, temporary homeless accommodation or supported housing. If you cannot come under the universal credit system, you must claim housing benefit to help with the cost of your rent. Chapter 11 explains who comes under the universal credit system.

How much help do you get?

The amount you get towards your rent in universal credit and housing benefit depends on all your circumstances, including the amount of income and savings you have, the size of your household, and also the size and type of property you rent.

If you have a private landlord, the amount you get is limited to a set figure, called the 'local housing allowance'. This sets amounts in your area for the size of property you are assessed as needing. Each local authority has its own rates for properties of different sizes, up to a maximum of four bedrooms. Check your local authority's rates at lha-direct.voa.gov.uk/search.aspx.

The local housing allowance means that if you are living in a property that is considered too big for you and your family, not all your rent is covered and you will have to make up the difference. If you are in rent arrears or facing eviction because of the shortfall, get advice.

You are allowed one bedroom for each of the following members of your family:

- a couple
- someone aged 16 or over
- two children under 16 of the same sex
- two children under 10 years old
- any other child
- a carer (or carers) providing overnight care for a disabled child or adult

You may be allowed an additional bedroom if, for example, you have a child with a disability, you are a couple but cannot share a room with your partner because of a disability, or if you are a foster carer.

EXAMPLE

Local housing allowance

Rosie lives with her three children – her son aged 10, and her two daughters aged five and two. She gets universal credit. They live in a three-bedroom private rented flat. The rent is £150 a week. Under the local housing allowance rules she is allowed one bedroom for herself, one for her son and one bedroom for her two daughters. The local housing allowance for a three-bedroom property in her area is £133 a week. Rosie gets a housing cost element in her universal credit of £133 a week, and has to find money from elsewhere to meet the shortfall in her rent.

If you live in a local authority or housing association property, the amount of help you can get with your rent in universal credit and housing benefit can also be restricted in a similar way. This is commonly known as the 'bedroom tax'. It only applies if you and your partner are under pension age.

The number of bedrooms you are allowed is calculated in the same way as for private rented property.

If you have one more bedroom than you are allowed, the amount of rent used to calculate your benefit is reduced by 14 per cent. If you have two or more additional bedrooms, it is reduced by 25 per cent.

What families say

Bedroom tax

'Our client lives in a three-bedroom house with the 11 year old and an 18 month old that she provides kinship care for. She is deemed as having an extra bedroom, even though she does not, so the bedroom tax has been applied. The client receives discretionary housing payments to make up the difference between the rent and her housing benefit, but she has to re-apply for it every year.' *Citizens Advice adviser*

If your universal credit/housing benefit is reduced in this way, you should apply for a discretionary housing payment from the local authority.

EXAMPLE

Bedroom tax

Sadie and her 17 year old daughter live in a two-bedroom housing association flat. Sadie gets housing benefit, which pays her rent of £80 a week in full. Her daughter moves out. Sadie now has a spare bedroom, so her housing benefit is reduced by 14 per cent of her rent. She now gets housing benefit of only £68.80 a week.

The amount of benefit you get to help you with your rent (whether you rent from a local authority, housing association or private landlord) is also reduced if you have a 'non-dependant' living with you. A 'non-dependant' is another adult, such as an adult son or daughter or another relative, who shares your home and who the government expects to be making a contribution to the rent. Some people do not count as non-dependants – eg, young people included in your benefit claim, joint tenants and lodgers.

An amount for each non-dependant is deducted from your benefit, even if you do not receive any contribution from that person. However, there are some situations in which no amount is deducted – eg, if you are getting the middle or highest rate of disability living allowance care component, or the personal independence payment daily living component.

You may also be eligible for an extra amount to help with certain service charges, such as some warden and caretaker services, communal lifts and entry phones.

3. Are you paying a mortgage?

If you are getting a means-tested benefit (universal credit, income support, income-based jobseeker's allowance, income-related employment and support allowance or pension credit) and you own your own home, you may be able to get a repayable loan to help with your mortgage interest payments.

You may also be eligible for an extra amount included in your benefit to help with certain service charges, such as some warden and caretaker services, communal lifts and entry phones.

However, if you are claiming universal credit, you do not get this help if you are doing any paid work, even if it is only for a few hours each week.

You do not usually get any help with your housing costs during the first nine months of your claim.

The amount of help with your mortgage is not based on what you pay, but is calculated by using a standard interest rate. The money to help with your mortgage is always paid directly to your lender, not to you.

You do not need to repay the loan (and the interest on the loan) until the property is sold or transferred to someone else. You should obtain financial advice before taking out the loan.

4. Can you get a discretionary housing payment?

Local authorities have the discretion to pay people additional payments if they are finding it difficult to pay their rent and certain other housing costs. These are called discretionary housing payments. To be eligible, you must be entitled to universal credit or housing benefit, and you must appear to need additional financial help. Because the payments are discretionary, it is up to the local authority whether or not to pay you, how much to pay you and for how long.

5. Can you get help with your council tax?

Council tax is a tax on the home you live in, and is paid to the local authority. In some cases, the home you live in may be exempt from council tax – eg, if everyone over 18 who lives there is a full-time student. In other cases, you can get a discount on your council tax – eg, if you live alone, or are a lone parent and no other adult lives in the property, you can get a discount of 25 per cent.

You may also be eligible for council tax reduction, which is administered by the local authority. You can get this if your income is low enough, and it may help to pay some, or all, of your council tax. Apply to your local authority.

6. Can you get help with fuel costs?

If you are on a low income or you receive a qualifying benefit, you may be entitled to help with fuel costs – eg, electricity and gas. You may be able to get energy efficiency assistance or reduced energy bills. You should contact the Energy Saving Trust, your local authority or your energy provider for further details of schemes you might be eligible for.

You can get a winter fuel payment if you have reached pension age. This is a one-off payment of £200, paid every winter. A higher rate is paid if you are 80 or over and a lower rate if you are in residential care or live with someone else.

In Scotland, from winter 2020, you can get child winter heating assistance if you are a family with a severely disabled child.

Further information

If you need housing advice, contact Shelter: 0808 800 4444.

Find out more about the Energy Saving Trust at energysavingtrust.org.uk.

Winter fuel payment helpline: 0800 731 0160 or see gov.uk/winter-fuel-payment.

Information on winter heating assistance is at cpag.org.uk/scotland/welfare-rights/scottish-benefits/winter-heating-assistance.

Chapter 7
Disability in the family

This chapter covers:

1. What help is available?

2. Do you or your partner have a disability?

3. Do you have a disabled child?

4. Are you caring for someone who is disabled?

5. Can you get help with transport?

6. How can you reduce your bills?

What you need to know

- If you have a disability you may be entitled to extra help from the social security system.

- If you care for a child or adult with a disability, you may be entitled to extra help.

- If you have a disability, or care for a person with a disability, it is a good idea to get a benefit check.

- Help is available for people who are either in or out of work.

- If you disagree with the result of an assessment of your disability, you often have a right to challenge the decision.

- If you live in Scotland, benefits for disabled people and carers are changing over the next few years.

1. What help is available?

There is additional help available if you, or a member of your family, have a long-term health condition or disability. These benefits acknowledge that there are additional costs of having a disability. Getting a disability benefit may mean your other benefit payments increase and may mean you can get help with travel costs and reduced bills. If you care for a disabled adult or child, you may be entitled to payments as a carer.

> Box A
> **Financial help if there is disability in the family: checklist**
> - personal independence payment
> - attendance allowance
> - disability living allowance
> - additional amounts in means-tested benefits
> - carer's allowance
> - national insurance credits
> - Motability scheme
> - blue badge parking
> - vehicle tax exemption or reduction
> - concessionary travel
> - NHS travel costs
> - council tax discounts and reduction
> - TV licence fee concessions
> - Christmas bonus
> - VAT exemption

2. Do you or your partner have a disability?

There are two main benefits for adults with a disability or long-term health condition. Which one you claim depends on your age.

- If you are aged 16 or over, you can claim personal independence payment. There is a 'mobility component' if you have particular mobility difficulties and a 'daily living component' if you have particular difficulties with daily living activities. Each component is paid at a standard or enhanced rate.

- If you have reached 'pension age', you can claim attendance allowance. There is a lower rate and a higher rate depending on how much care you need. You do not need to switch to attendance allowance at age 65 if you are already getting personal independence payment. Instead, you can stay on and renew your existing benefit.

- If you live in Scotland, personal independence payment is being replaced by a new adult disability payment. For new claims, this was meant to start in 2021 but may be later because of coronavirus. Attendance allowance is being replaced in Scotland by a new pension age disability payment.

Your entitlement does not depend on how much income or savings you have, and you do not need to have paid national insurance contributions.

What families say

Personal independence payment

'Because I'm getting personal independence payment, it sort of takes the burden off. Since we got the benefits all sort of settled it is a big improvement. I'm not struggling now. I don't struggle now. I have struggled in the past. Anything that is helping any child living in poverty, anything that is going to put extra money into the family budget, is a good thing, is a positive thing.'
Disabled single father with disabled son

There is a third benefit, disability living allowance, which is now just for children. Adults who have been getting disability living allowance are invited to claim personal independence payment instead (see Box B).

EXAMPLES

Benefits for disability

Martha is 45. She had a stroke three months ago which has restricted her movement down her right-hand side. She is unable to walk and needs help with washing and getting dressed. She is entitled to the daily living component and the mobility component of personal independence payment.

Ildiko is 67. She has arthritis which particularly affects her legs, hips and hands. She needs help getting dressed, washed and using the toilet. She is entitled to attendance allowance.

A claim for personal independence payment is made over the phone. You are then usually asked to complete a 'How your disability affects you' form, on which you can provide details of your care needs and the difficulties you have getting around. You may also be asked to attend an assessment in person.

A claim for attendance allowance is made on a paper form, available online or by calling the attendance allowance helpline. This form allows you to provide details of your care needs. Some people who claim attendance allowance are asked to attend an assessment in person.

What CPAG says

Supporting information

Providing additional information, such as medical reports or supporting statements, can help ensure that the correct decision is made about your benefit entitlement. This additional information should be sent to the office dealing with your claim. You should check that any medical evidence you submit is relevant and supports your application. Supporting statements can come from someone who cares for you, a member of your family or any professionals who work with you or your family. Make a copy of the form and the evidence before you send it to the Department for Work and Pensions.

If you go into hospital or a care home, some or all of your disability benefits may end after a period of time. You should tell the Department for Work and Pensions as soon as you can to avoid having to repay any overpaid benefit.

If you have a terminal illness, you may be automatically entitled to the personal independence payment daily living component or attendance allowance. You still need to make a claim. Which one you claim depends on your age.

Box B
Transfers to personal independence payment

If you are over 16 and were under 65 on 8 April 2013 and currently receive disability living allowance, at some point the Department for Work and Pensions will write to you and invite you to claim personal independence payment.

If you do not claim personal independence payment, your disability living allowance award stops. If you make a claim for personal independence payment, your disability living allowance award continues until your eligibility for personal independence payment has been decided. You should check any letters you get from the Department for Work and Pensions. You have a limited amount of time to make a claim before your disability living allowance award ends.

If you get disability living allowance or personal independence payment, you are exempt from the 'benefit cap'. This is the maximum amount of social security benefits that someone getting universal credit or housing benefit can receive. There is more on the benefit cap in Chapter 10.

Do you qualify for additional help?

Getting attendance allowance, disability living allowance or personal independence payment means you can qualify for other kinds of help. If you are currently getting another social security benefit, the amount you receive could increase, or getting a disability benefit could mean that you become entitled to one of the benefits below for the first time. Contact the office dealing with that benefit as soon as possible to tell it that you are getting a disability benefit.

- If you get universal credit and you are over 'pension age', you may be able to have a 'limited capability for work-related activity element' included in your benefit.

- If you get income support, income-based jobseeker's allowance, income-related employment and support allowance or housing benefit, you may be able to have a 'disability premium', 'enhanced disability premium' or 'severe disability premium' included in your benefit.

- If you get working tax credit, you may be able to have a 'disabled worker element' or 'severe disability element' included.

EXAMPLE

Additional amounts

Donna gets income-related employment and support allowance because she is unable to work. She is awarded the enhanced rate of the daily living component of personal independence payment. Because she lives alone, she is entitled to a severe disability premium in her employment and support allowance. She contacts the Department for Work and Pensions and is told this will be added – her entitlement is backdated to the date her personal independence payment started.

3. Do you have a disabled child?

There are benefits and other support available to help with the extra costs of having a disabled child. Because all children, particularly babies, need a lot of care, not all children with a disability or health condition qualify. If benefit is refused for a young child, a later claim may be successful.

Disability living allowance

If your child has a disability, you may be able to claim disability living allowance for her/him.

If s/he needs more care or supervision than most children of her/his age, s/he may be able to get the disability living allowance 'care component'. This is paid at one of three rates and can be claimed from the age of three months.

If your child is unable to walk or requires additional supervision when walking outside, s/he may be able to get the 'mobility component'. This is paid at one of two rates. Your child must be at least three years old to get the higher rate and at least five to get the lower rate.

EXAMPLE

Disability living allowance for children

Brian is 14. He has epilepsy. Despite his medication, he has regular seizures. His epilepsy means he requires supervision throughout the day to ensure that he does not injure himself when he has seizures. He is entitled to the care component of disability living allowance.

If a child is under 16, a parent or other main carer will be authorised to act as her/his 'appointee'. This means, for example, that you are responsible for completing the relevant forms and making claims on behalf of your child.

If you live in Scotland, a new benefit is planned to be introduced in 2021 to replace disability living allowance. When it is introduced, if you make a new claim for your child, it will be for child disability payment instead of disability living allowance.

If your child receives disability living allowance, you may be entitled to additional amounts in your universal credit, housing benefit and child tax credit, or this may mean you become entitled to these benefits for the first time. Contact the office dealing with your benefit as soon as possible to tell it that your child is getting disability living allowance.

EXAMPLE

Additional amounts

Jenny is a lone parent and gets universal credit. Her five year old son has been diagnosed with autism and needs additional care. She applies for disability living allowance for him and gets the middle rate of the care component. She can now get an additional amount included in her universal credit. She should tell the Department for Work and Pensions that her son is now getting disability living allowance.

If your child gets disability living allowance, you are exempt from the 'benefit cap'. This is the maximum amount of social security benefits that someone getting universal credit or housing benefit can receive. There is more on the benefit cap in Chapter 10.

What happens when your child is 16?

If you are getting disability living allowance for your child, s/he will usually be contacted by the Department for Work and Pensions and invited to claim personal independence payment when s/he turns 16. If this happens, s/he must claim personal independence payment, otherwise her/his disability living allowance will end. However, not all children who are entitled to disability living allowance are entitled to personal independence payment. If your child's personal independence payment claim is turned down, s/he can challenge that decision.

If your child is in hospital, s/he should remain on disability living allowance, even after s/he turns 16, until s/he leaves hospital. If your child has a terminal illness, s/he should remain on disability living allowance when s/he turns 16 – s/he does not need to claim personal independence payment.

If you are getting disability living allowance for your child and you live in Scotland, your child will not be contacted by the Department for Work and Pensions and invited to claim personal independance payment; instead her/his disability living allowance will continue until s/he is 18, unless s/he chooses to claim personal independance payment.

When your child turns 16, s/he may also be able to claim universal credit in her/his own right. Alternatively, you may be able to continue to claim child benefit, child tax credit or an additional amount in your universal credit for her/him. Get a benefit check so you know which option would give your family the most income.

The Family Fund

The Family Fund is a charity providing grants to buy specific items to help care for a child under 18 who has a severe disability or a serious illness. You can apply if you get a 'means-tested benefit' like universal credit or child tax credit. Even if you do not get one of these benefits, you can still apply but any help you are entitled to depends on your household income. You can find out more at familyfund.org.uk.

4. Are you caring for someone who is disabled?

If you care for someone who gets the 'daily living component' of personal independence payment, the middle or highest rate of the 'care component' of disability living allowance or attendance allowance, you may be able to get carer's allowance.

To be eligible you must provide care for 35 hours a week and not be 'gainfully employed'. This means that you must earn less than a certain amount. Only one person can receive carer's allowance for a disabled person, so if you have a disabled child, you and your partner must choose who should claim.

If you are entitled to carer's allowance, you may also get a 'carer element' in your universal credit or an additional amount in your jobseeker's allowance, employment and support allowance, housing benefit, income support or pension credit. Contact the office dealing with your benefit as soon as possible to tell it that you are caring for a disabled person. **Note:** you may also get additional amounts in your universal credit if you care for someone but are not entitled to carer's allowance – eg, because your earnings are too high.

Getting carer's allowance, or caring for someone, could mean that you become entitled to universal credit or pension credit for the first time. Chapter 11 explains who can claim universal credit and pension credit.

EXAMPLE

Carer's allowance

Sam and Dave have a disabled child who gets the highest rate of the disability living allowance care component. Both Sam and Dave provide care for more than 35 hours a week. Dave does not work so they decide that he will claim carer's allowance as the main carer of their child. He gets carer's allowance. The couple then get an additional amount (a carer element) in their universal credit.

If your universal credit includes a carer element or you get income support as a carer, you do not need to look for work or attend any interviews about work. There is more information about this in Chapter 5.

If your universal credit includes a carer element or you get carer's allowance, you are also exempt from the 'benefit cap'. This is the maximum amount of social security benefits that someone getting housing benefit or universal credit can receive. There is more on the benefit cap in Chapter 10.

If you live in Scotland, you are entitled to an additional carer's allowance supplement if you are getting carer's allowance on specified dates. This is a lump sum of £230.10 that is paid automatically once a year.

In Scotland, young carers aged at least 16 and under 19, who care for a disabled person, may be eligible for a young carer grant of £305.01. Chapter 11 explains who can apply and how to make an application.

What CPAG says

The effect on the disabled person's benefits

Claiming carer's allowance can reduce the benefit income of the person you are caring for. If the person you care for gets income-based jobseeker's allowance, income-related employment and support allowance, income support or pension credit, s/he may receive an additional amount in her/his benefit because s/he is severely disabled (known as a 'severe disability premium'). This premium will be removed if you claim carer's allowance as her/his carer. If the person you care for gets one of these benefits, before you make a claim for carer's allowance get a benefit check to ensure s/he does not lose out.

National insurance credits

If you care for someone for at least 20 hours a week, you may be entitled to national insurance credits. These help fill any gaps in your contribution record (eg, because you are not in paid work), and so help to protect your future entitlement to benefits – eg, your state pension. If you receive carer's allowance, you get these credits automatically. If you do not receive carer's allowance, you can claim the credits from the Department for Work and Pensions on Form CC1.

5. Can you get help with transport?

Motability

If you get the enhanced rate of personal independence payment 'mobility component' or the higher rate of disability living allowance mobility component and your award has at least 12 months left to run, you can get assistance with the cost of buying or hiring a car through the Motability scheme. To apply, contact Motability, the charity that runs the scheme, on 0300 456 4566.

Blue badge parking

If you get the enhanced rate of personal independence payment 'mobility component' or the higher rate of disability living allowance mobility component, you can get a blue badge from your local authority, which allows you more flexibility in where you can park. Even if you do not get these benefits, you may still be able to get a blue badge if you have a disability which affects your walking or driving. Apply online at gov.uk/apply-blue-badge. If you are refused a blue badge, ask the local authority to reconsider its decision.

Vehicle tax reduction

You can get a reduction or exemption from vehicle tax for one car that is registered in the disabled person's name or in the name of a nominated driver, provided it is used by, or for, the disabled person. When you apply for vehicle tax, claim a reduction or exemption if you get any of the following benefits:

- the higher rate of disability living allowance 'mobility component'
- the enhanced rate of personal independence payment mobility component
- the standard rate of personal independence payment mobility component (you pay half the tax)
- armed forces independence payment
- war pensioners' mobility supplement

Concessionary travel

If you have difficulty getting about, you may be entitled to a concessionary travel card that allows free or subsidised access to public transport. Concessionary travel schemes are administered by local authorities. Contact your local authority for details of what is available.

You may also qualify for a disabled person's railcard. This gives you and a travelling companion 30 per cent off rail fares. For details of who is eligible and how to apply, see disabledpersons-railcard.co.uk or phone 0345 605 0525.

NHS travel costs

You may be entitled to help with paying for your travel to medical appointments if you are accompanying your child and your income is low enough.

6. How can you reduce your bills?

You may be able to reduce your council tax bill in one or more of the following ways.

- You can get a reduction in the amount of council tax you must pay if you (or anyone you live with) have a disability and you have space in your home to enable you to use a wheelchair in your home, or you need an extra room, bathroom or kitchen to meet your disability needs.

- Your council tax bill is based on the assumption that two adults live in the property and a discount is given if there is only one. You can be discounted in this way if you (or anyone you live with) are 'severely mentally impaired' – eg, if you have Alzheimer's disease or have had a stroke. You may also be able to get a discount if you are caring for someone (not your partner) in your home – eg, an adult son or daughter or another relative or friend.

- If your income is low, you may get help with your bill from your local authority's council tax reduction scheme. Chapter 6 has more on this.

If you have a council tax bill to pay, check whether any of these might apply and make sure the local authority knows that you or someone you live with gets disability living allowance, personal independence payment, attendance allowance or carer's allowance. You may get more help.

TV licence

If you are blind (severely sight impaired), you can apply for a 50 per cent concession on your television licence fee. The licence must be in the name of the person who is blind. If you live with someone who is blind, the TV licence can be transferred into her/his name to allow the discount to apply. This includes children who are blind. For further details and how to apply, see gov.uk/free-discount-tv-licence.

Christmas bonus

If you get one of a number of benefits, including personal independence payment, disability living allowance or attendance allowance, you should get a £10 Christmas bonus. This is paid automatically. If you do not get the bonus, contact the Department for Work and Pensions.

VAT

If you are disabled or have a long-term illness, you are not charged VAT on any products designed or adapted for your own use, or for their installation or repair. For details of eligibility and how to get the products VAT free, see gov.uk/financial-help-disabled/vat-relief or speak to the supplier.

What CPAG says

Poverty is bad for your health

Living on a low income makes it more likely that you or your child will have a long-term physical or mental illness. Bad housing, damp or cold homes can damage a child's health and their educational achievement. Not everyone knows what financial support is available and it is easy to miss out on help that can make a real difference. If anyone in the family has a disability, or cares for a person with a disability, it is always a good idea to get a benefit check.

Further information

Carers UK has a helpline for carers: 0808 808 7777, carersuk.org.

Contact has a helpline for families with a disabled child: 0808 808 3555, contact.org.uk.

Chapter 8
Bereavement in the family

This chapter covers:

1. What help is available?

2. Who should you contact?

3. Was the person who has died claiming benefits?

4. Were you caring for the person who has died?

5. Was the person who has died included in your benefit claim?

6. Can you get help with the funeral costs?

7. Can you get any benefits for your bereavement?

8. What other help is there?

What you need to know

- If you have a bereavement in the family, this is a change of circumstances that affects your benefit entitlement.

- If any of your benefits include an amount for someone who has now died, these should be reassessed. If the person who has died was getting benefits, these must be cancelled.

- You may be entitled to help with the cost of the funeral and may qualify for other benefits.

1. What help is available?

When there is a bereavement in the family, it can be an emotional and stressful time. You may be worried about money. Get advice if you are unsure what you should do about cancelling the benefits of the person who has died, or if you want to know what help you may now be able to get.

Box A
Financial help for bereavement: checklist
- funeral payments
- bereavement benefits
- means-tested benefits

2. Who should you contact?

If you have had a bereavement in the family, you should report the death to the relevant government departments as soon as you can, to avoid any overpayment of benefit. There is a service that can help with this called 'Tell Us Once', which is available in most parts of the country. When you register the death with your local authority, the registrar will tell you whether the service is available where you live, and explain what to do.

If Tell Us Once is not available, you must contact each government department separately:

- for most benefits, contact the Department for Work and Pensions Bereavement Service on 0800 731 0469 (Relay UK dial 18001 first; textphone 0800 731 0464)
- for child benefit, call the Child Benefit Helpline on 0300 200 3100 (Relay UK dial 18001 first)
- for tax credits, call the Tax Credit Helpline on 0345 300 3900 (Relay UK dial 18001 first)
- for carer's allowance, contact the Carer's Allowance Unit on 0800 731 0297 (Relay UK dial 18001 first; textphone 0800 731 0317)
- contact your local authority to deal with housing benefit, council tax, blue badge parking permits and any social services (eg, meals on wheels) the person was receiving

3. Was the person who has died claiming benefit?

Any benefits or tax credits that were being paid to the person who has died must be cancelled by the Department for Work and Pensions or HM Revenue and Customs. These include benefits paid because of her/his disability (such as disability living allowance, personal independence payment or attendance allowance) as well as tax credits and other benefits (such as universal credit, employment and support allowance and jobseeker's allowance).

The 'Tell Us Once' service should deal with this – otherwise, you should contact the Department for Work and Pensions Bereavement Service.

If it is your partner who has died and s/he was claiming child benefit for your child(ren), this claim must be cancelled. You can then make a new claim in your name, provided you are responsible for the child(ren). Contact the Child Benefit Office.

If your partner was claiming housing benefit for the family, this claim must also be cancelled. Contact the local authority. You will usually need to claim universal credit as most people cannot now claim housing benefit. Chapter 11 explains who comes under the universal credit system as well as who can make a new claim for housing benefit.

4. Were you caring for the person who has died?

If you were caring for the person who has died and getting carer's allowance, you should tell the Department for Work and Pensions Carer's Allowance Unit about the death. Your carer's allowance continues for eight weeks from the date of death, then stops.

If you have been getting universal credit on the basis of being a carer with a 'carer element' included, tell the Department for Work and Pensions, so that your benefit can be reassessed. The carer element continues to be paid for the remainder of the monthly 'assessment period' in which the death occurs, and for the next two complete months, then stops. When this happens you may be expected to do more things to find work. Chapter 5 has more information on this.

If you were getting income support as a carer, you must also tell the income support section at the Department for Work and Pensions. The contact details are on the letters you have from it. Your income support continues for eight weeks then stops, so you may need to think about claiming universal credit at this point.

Note: you can continue to receive income support if you come into one of the other groups of people who can claim it – eg, if you are a lone parent with a child under five years old. If this is the case, you must still report the death of the person you were caring for, and have your award reassessed to take account of the new basis for your claim. The amount you are paid will then be reduced, as the 'carer premium' will no longer be included in your award.

5. Was the person who has died included in your benefit claim?

If your partner or child has died, any benefits you get that include amounts for her/him must be reassessed – these include universal credit, housing benefit, working tax credit, child tax credit and child benefit.

The amount you are paid for her/him in your universal credit continues for the remainder of that monthly 'assessment period' and for the next two complete months.

If your partner has died and you were claiming tax credits jointly with her/him, you must end that claim. You will then usually need to claim universal credit.

If your child has died, your child benefit and child tax credit must be reassessed. Your benefit continues to be paid for her/him for eight weeks, and then stops. If s/he was your only child, your award ends altogether.

6. Can you get help with the funeral costs?

In England and Wales, if your partner, child, or family member or close friend, has died, you may qualify for a **funeral expenses payment** to help with the costs of her/his funeral.

To qualify, you must be getting a qualifying benefit (Box B).

Box B
Qualifying benefits for funeral expenses payment and funeral support payment
- universal credit
- income support
- income-based jobseeker's allowance
- income-related employment and support allowance
- housing benefit
- child tax credit
- working tax credit, which includes a disabled worker or severe disability element
- pension credit

Unless it is your partner or child who has died, you must show that it is reasonable for you to accept responsibility for the funeral expenses. This means that you may have to show that there is no one who was closer to the person who has died and who could be expected to take responsibility, such as her/his partner, parent, son or daughter. You must also have accepted liability for the costs, not just simply started making the arrangements.

The person who has died must have been living in the UK when s/he died. Usually, the funeral must also take place in the UK, although funerals in European Economic Area countries or Switzerland may also qualify in some circumstances. You may not qualify if you are not a British national.

You can claim at any time from the date of death up to six months after the date of the funeral. If you have claimed one of the qualifying benefits but it has not yet been awarded, the Department for Work and Pensions may postpone making a decision until your claim for a qualifying benefit has been decided. Alternatively, you may be refused a funeral expenses payment. If this happens, you can reclaim within three months of being awarded the 'qualifying benefit'.

If you qualify for a payment, you are entitled to a payment to cover:

- the costs of a burial plot and burial fees (but not the cost of burying ashes following a cremation)
- cremation fees
- the costs of any documentation needed to release any assets
- certain transport costs
- up to a further £1,000 for any other funeral expenses – eg, a funeral director's fees, religious costs and flowers

If you live in Scotland, **funeral support payment** is a one-off grant to help with the costs of a funeral in the UK (or sometimes elsewhere in Europe). Usually the person with the closest family relationship who takes responsibility for the funeral can apply for a payment. To qualify, you must be getting a qualifying benefit (Box B). The payment covers the full cost of some of the fees such as cremation and burial fees, and £1,000 towards other expenses. Apply to Social Security Scotland at mygov.scot or by phoning 0800 182 2222.

In England, you may be entitled to a payment from the children's funeral fund if the funeral is for a child under 18 or a baby stillborn after the 24th week of pregnancy. The funeral must take place in England and you must be responsible for organising it, though the funeral director usually applies for the payment. The payment covers burial or cremation fees and an amount for a coffin. You can also apply for a funeral expenses payment for other funeral costs. You do not have to get a 'qualifying benefit' or have a low income to get a children's funeral fund payment.

7. Can you get any benefits for your bereavement?

If you were married to, or in a civil partnership with, the person who has died, you may qualify for bereavement support payment or widowed parent's allowance.

- If your spouse or civil partner died on or after 6 April 2017, you may be entitled to bereavement support payment.

- If s/he died before then, you may qualify for widowed parent's allowance instead.

Unmarried partners have not been able to claim bereavement benefits. There are plans to change the rules so that if you have children and your partner has died, you will be able to claim bereavement support payment or widowed parent's allowance.

Bereaved parents of children under 18 may be entitled to statutory parental bereavement pay from their employer. It is paid for two weeks with your wages. There are details about this in Chapter 11.

How are your other benefits affected?

The monthly payments of bereavement support payment do not affect any 'means-tested benefits' (eg, universal credit, income support, income-related employment and support allowance, income-based jobseeker's allowance and housing benefit) you may be getting. They can be paid alongside these benefits without leading to any reduction. There is also an initial one-off lump sum payment, which does not count as your capital for these benefits, provided it is spent within 12 months.

Getting widowed parent's allowance means that the amount of universal credit (and some other benefits) you are paid is reduced. You should tell the department which pays your benefit so it can be reassessed.

Bereavement support payment is not included when working out the total amount of social security benefits you get for the 'benefit cap'. This is the maximum amount of certain social security benefits that someone getting universal credit or housing benefit can receive. Widowed parent's allowance is included. There is more on the benefit cap in Chapter 10.

Statutory parental bereavement pay is paid with your wages. You may be getting a benefit, such as universal credit, where the amount you get depends on the level of your wages. Your universal credit amount adjusts automatically so there should be no need for you to report getting statutory parental bereavement pay. However, if you get housing benefit, you should tell the local authority housing benefit section if your wages change.

8. What other help is there?

If your partner has died, check whether you can claim universal credit to help with your housing and living costs. Universal credit can also include amounts for children and childcare as well as for ill health, disability and carers.

You may also qualify for council tax reduction, if your low income means you cannot afford to pay your council tax. Ask your local council about this and other discounts available to you.

Further information

For what to do when someone dies, see gov.uk/after-a-death.

Chapter 9
Children in care

What you need to know

- If your child goes into care, your benefit entitlement may change almost immediately.

- If you are a 'kinship carer', you may be entitled to family benefits for the child you care for.

- Getting good advice as soon as possible is crucial to prevent overpayments and underpayments.

1. What help is available?

If a child is unable to live with her/his birth family, s/he may go to live with other family members or friends. This is often called 'kinship care' or 'family and friends care'. Alternatively, s/he may be placed by the local authority with a foster carer or in a residential establishment. Money worries can arise for the birth family, for kinship carers and for foster carers. It is important to know which benefits should be paid in these situations to avoid being underpaid or overpaid.

2. Has your child gone into care?

Some of your benefits and tax credits may change if your child goes into care – eg, if s/he goes to stay in a residential unit or secure accommodation, or s/he has been placed with foster carers. You may have agreed to this happening or it may be because of a legal order. Your child may be described as being 'looked after away from home', 'looked after and accommodated' or in the care of the local authority.

Note: the following changes do not apply if your child is in residential accommodation provided *solely* because of her/his disability or because her/his health would be significantly impaired if the accommodation were not provided.

- **Child benefit.** This stops after your child has been in care for eight weeks in a row. Notify the Child Benefit Office if your child has been looked after away from home for eight weeks. The local authority should use Form CH193 to notify the Child Benefit Office when a child comes into care, but it is still your responsibility to do so.

- **Universal credit.** The 'child element' in your universal credit stops when your child is in care. If you are getting the disabled child element or any help with childcare costs for her/him, these also stop. The amount you are allowed to earn before your universal credit starts being affected (your 'work allowance') may also change. If you are in rented accommodation, the amount included in your universal credit for housing costs is calculated as if the child were still living with you for the first six months of her/his being in care. Notify the Department for Work and Pensions immediately.

- **Tax credits.** You stop counting as responsible for your child as soon as s/he is in care. This means that your child tax credit for her/him stops and your working tax credit may also be affected. Notify the Tax Credit Office immediately.

- **Income support and jobseeker's allowance.** Your child stops counting as part of your household as soon as s/he is in care. If you are claiming income support as a lone parent, you can no longer do so, unless you have another child under five years old who is still at home with you. If you are still getting amounts in your income support and jobseeker's allowance for the child in care, these stop. You should notify the Department for Work and Pensions immediately.

- **Housing benefit**. Your child stops counting as part of your household as soon as s/he is in care. This means that your housing benefit no longer includes amounts for her/him. Your benefit may also be reduced if you are considered to need fewer bedrooms. Chapter 6 has more information about this. Tell your local authority housing benefit office immediately.

- **Disability living allowance**. If your child is living with a foster carer, both the 'mobility component' and the 'care component' continue to be paid. If s/he is in a residential unit/school, the care component stops after four weeks. If your child is getting disability living allowance care component, notify the Disability Benefit Centre immediately. If your child's disability living allowance was paid to you (as her/his 'appointee'), this stops if s/he is expected to be in care for more than 12 weeks. The foster carer or local authority becomes the appointee instead. Notify the Disability Benefit Centre.

- **Carer's allowance**. Your carer's allowance stops if you are no longer caring for your disabled child for 35 hours or more a week, or because her/his disability living allowance care component has stopped being paid. If you are getting universal credit, the 'carer element' stops as soon as you are no longer caring for the child. If you get an amount for being a carer in another 'means-tested benefit', such as housing benefit or income support, this stops eight weeks after your entitlement to carer's allowance stops. If you are claiming carer's allowance for looking after your child, notify the Carer's Allowance Unit immediately. If you get any means-tested benefits, tell the Department for Work and Pensions and/or local authority that your carer's allowance has stopped.

- **Scottish child payment**. If the child goes into care, you stop getting Scottish child payment when you stop being responsible for the child and/or you stop getting a qualifying benefit. If you get child benefit for the child, this will be at the same time as your child benefit stops. Chapter 11 has information about Scottish child payment and when you are responsible for a child.

Does your child come home for some of the time?

There are different rules if your child is in care but comes home for some of the time – eg, at weekends.

- **Child benefit**. You can get child benefit for any week when your child comes home for seven consecutive nights, or for any nights immediately following the first seven, or if s/he comes home on a regular basis for at least two consecutive nights each week. Notify the Child Benefit Office of any nights your child spends at home. If you stopped getting child benefit when s/he went into care, you should make a new claim.

- **Universal credit**. When your child comes home, your universal credit should be adjusted to include the 'child element', even if s/he is still being looked after by the local authority. However, if s/he is only coming home for a brief period, your universal credit may not increase because of the way the 'assessment periods' work. For example, if your child comes home and then returns to care within the same assessment period, your universal credit will not be increased. To be on the safe side, you should notify the Department for Work and Pensions each time your child comes home.

- **Tax credits**. Tax credits are not paid for the days your child spends at home while s/he is still formally looked after away from home.

- **Income support and jobseeker's allowance**. If you have continued to get a 'personal allowance' for another child in the family while your child has been looked after away from home, you can get an increase in this for the days your child spends at home. If you are still getting amounts in your income support or jobseeker's allowance for a child, notify the Department for Work and Pensions of any nights your child spends at home. If you no longer get any personal allowance for a child in your income support or jobseeker's allowance, you are not paid this increase for days your child spends at home.

- **Housing benefit.** If your child comes home for part of the week, the local authority can calculate your housing benefit as if s/he were home for the whole week if it is reasonable to do so, taking into account the nature and frequency of her/his visits. Notify the housing benefit office of any nights your child spends at home.

- **Disability living allowance.** If your child's 'care component' in her/his disability living allowance has stopped because s/he is in residential care, it can be paid for any days s/he is at home. The day s/he comes home and the day s/he goes back count as days at home. Notify the Disability Benefit Centre of any days the child spends at home.

- **Carer's allowance.** If your child is disabled and gets the disability living allowance 'care component' (paid at the middle or highest rate), you may be able to get carer's allowance if s/he starts coming home for some of the time and you are caring for her/him for 35 hours or more a week (Sunday to Saturday). The hours do not have to be spread across the whole week. You may need to make a new claim. If you are getting any 'means-tested benefits', or if you think you may be entitled because you are now getting carer's allowance, tell the Department for Work and Pensions and/or housing benefit office that carer's allowance has started.

- **Scottish child payment.** If your Scottish child payment for a child has stopped because s/he is in care, it should start being paid again once you are responsible for her/him again; this is likely to be when child benefit becomes payable again.

Note: you may have to claim universal credit instead of tax credits, income support, jobseeker's allowance and housing benefit when your child returns to live with you. Chapter 11 explains who comes under the universal credit system.

3. Are you a foster carer?

If you are looking after a child under 'public fostering' arrangements, you are excluded from claiming most family-related benefits for that child. Instead, you should be receiving a fostering payment from the local authority or the fostering agency which has arranged the foster placement.

- **Child benefit.** You cannot claim child benefit for a child you are fostering.

- **Universal credit.** You cannot include a foster child in your universal credit claim – s/he does not count as your dependant. This means you do not get a 'child element' for her/him and cannot get any help with your childcare costs for that child included in your universal credit. When the local authority looks at how many bedrooms you are allowed for the 'housing costs element', a child you are fostering is not included. You are allowed one additional room because you are a foster carer, regardless of how many children you are fostering. None of the payments you get for fostering count as income. If you are the main foster carer for a child aged under one, you do not have any 'work-related requirements' in your 'claimant commitment'. If the child is over one but under 16, you may be expected to go for 'work-focused interviews'.

- **Tax credits.** You cannot claim child tax credit for a child you are fostering, but you may be able to get working tax credit on the basis that you are a self-employed foster carer.

- **Income support and jobseeker's allowance.** If you are single and fostering a child under 16, you may be able to get income support. Any payment you get for fostering does not count as income for income support and jobseeker's allowance, although if you are paid a 'retainer' when you are not looking after any children, this counts as income.

- **Housing benefit.** A child you are fostering is not included in your housing benefit award – s/he does not count as your dependant. When the local authority looks at how many bedrooms you are allowed and whether your rent should be restricted, a child you are fostering is not included. You are allowed one additional room because you are a foster carer, regardless of how many children you are fostering. Any payment you get for fostering does not count as income for housing benefit, although if you are paid a retainer when you are not looking after any children, this counts as income if you are under 'pension age'.

- **Disability living allowance and personal independence payment.** If the child you care for is entitled to disability living allowance or personal independence payment, s/he can receive it while in foster care and you can be the 'appointee' (and be paid the benefit on the child's behalf).

- **Carer's allowance.** If the child you care for gets disability living allowance 'care component' paid at the middle or highest rate (or the 'daily living component' of personal independence payment), you can get carer's allowance provided you satisfy the other conditions of entitlement.

- **Scottish child payment.** Foster carers cannot get Scottish child payment for a child they are fostering. This is because they do not count as 'responsible' for the child for the purposes of Scottish child payment. Chapter 11 has information about Scottish child payment and when you are responsible for a child.

EXAMPLE

Housing benefit

Naya lives in a four-bedroom housing association house and with three children she is fostering. She is treated as needing two bedrooms – one for herself and one additional room because she is a foster carer.

4. Are you looking after a child under a kinship care arrangement?

You may be looking after a child who is not able to live with her/his parents. You may be a relative (eg, a grandparent) or a friend of the family. This is often called 'kinship care' (or 'family and friends care'). This may be a formal arrangement made through the courts or, in Scotland, the children's hearing system, or sometimes it is less formal and arranged within the family.

A child in kinship care may or may not be 'looked after' by the local authority. If the child is looked after, this affects which benefits you can claim. If you are not sure whether the child is looked after, ask her/his social worker, if s/he has one, or the local authority.

Is the child looked after by the local authority?

If the child you are caring for is 'looked after' by the local authority, this affects the benefits and tax credits you can claim. You are treated in a similar way to a foster carer, although there are some exceptions.

- **Child benefit.** If the child you care for is looked after and has been placed with you by the local authority and the local authority is paying you under specific legislation, you cannot get child benefit for her/him. There are some exceptions to this in Scotland, because local authorities have a choice about which legal powers to use to make payments to kinship carers and some types of payment do not prevent you getting child benefit.

- **Universal credit.** If the child is looked after by the local authority, you do not get a 'child element' in your universal credit, unless you have legal parental rights or responsibilities for her/him. Because you do not get the child element, you also do not get help with any childcare costs you have for the child. You should be exempt from looking for work until the child is 16 or s/he no longer counts as looked after, whichever comes first. When the Department for Work and Pensions looks at how many bedrooms you are allowed for the 'housing costs element', a looked-after child you are caring for is not included. You are allowed one extra room, regardless of how many looked-after children you care for.

- **Tax credits.** If the child you care for is looked after by the local authority, and the local authority is making a payment to you for accommodation and/or maintenance, you cannot get child tax credit for the child. In Scotland, some local authority payments to kinship carers are not for accommodation or maintenance – if you are in this situation, you may be able to get child tax credit. If you are caring for a looked-after child, you may be able to get working tax credit as a self-employed carer.

EXAMPLE

Housing costs element of universal credit

Beth is aged 50 and single. She cares for her three grandchildren (two girls, aged five and seven, and a boy aged 10). This is a kinship care arrangement and all three children are looked after by the local authority. Beth lives in a housing association house with three bedrooms. When her housing costs element is calculated, she is assessed as needing one bedroom for herself and one extra bedroom because she is a kinship carer of a looked-after child. Because she is only assessed as needing two bedrooms, the bedroom tax restricts the amount of rent that will be covered by the housing costs element of her universal credit.

Beth could claim a discretionary housing payment to cover the shortfall or ask the local authority for help.

- **Income support and income-based jobseeker's allowance.** Being a kinship carer of a looked-after child can affect your income support and income-based jobseeker's allowance in a number of ways. For example, if you do not have a partner and the child you are caring for is under 16, you can get income support on this basis.
- **Housing benefit.** The child you are caring for is not treated as part of your household for housing benefit purposes, even though s/he

lives with you. This can affect your housing benefit in a number of ways:

- Your housing benefit 'applicable amount' does not include an amount for the child.
- If you are living in private rented accommodation, your housing benefit is probably calculated using the 'local housing allowance'. This is based partly on how many bedrooms you are considered to need (known as the 'size criteria'). The size criteria does not include a looked-after child in kinship care. However, you are allowed one extra room in the size criteria because you are a kinship carer of a looked-after child. Even if you are caring for more than one looked-after child, you only get one extra room in the size criteria.
- If you are under 'pension age' and you live in local authority or housing association accommodation, you may be affected by the 'bedroom tax'. This is because a looked-after child in kinship care is not 'counted' when deciding whether or not you are under-occupying your home. However, you are allowed one extra room in the size criteria because you are a kinship carer of a looked-after child. Even if you are caring for more than one looked-after child, you only get one extra room in the size criteria.

- **Disability living allowance.** If the child you care for gets disability living allowance, you can apply to become the 'appointee' and receive the disability living allowance on behalf of the child. If you believe the child should be getting disability living allowance, you can make the claim.

- **Carer's allowance.** If the child you care for gets disability living allowance 'care component' at the middle or highest rate, you may be able to claim carer's allowance.

- **Scottish child payment.** You should be able to get Scottish child payment for the child, providing you are on one of the 'qualifying benefits'. Chapter 11 has details about Scottish child payment.

Box A
How do local authority payments affect your benefits?

As a kinship carer of a looked-after child, you will probably be receiving a regular payment from the local authority. This payment should be disregarded for benefits and tax credits.

What if the child is not looked after by the local authority?

If the child you care for is not looked after by the local authority, you should be able to claim any of the benefits or tax credits a family would usually get, providing you satisfy the normal rules. This includes child benefit and the 'child element' of universal credit. If you live in Scotland, it may also include Scottish child payment. It may include child tax credit and benefits like income support and housing benefit if you are already on one or more of these benefits and have not yet claimed universal credit.

There are some problems that may arise because you are claiming benefit as a kinship carer.

Box B
How do local authority payments affect your benefits?

As a kinship carer of a non-looked-after child, you may be receiving a regular payment from the local authority – eg, a special guardianship allowance, child arrangement order allowance or, in Scotland, a kinship care allowance. Generally, all these types of payments are disregarded for benefits and tax credits.

Box C
Special rules for universal credit and child tax credit

In some circumstances, you can only get amounts in your universal credit or child tax credit for a maximum of two children. This is known as the 'two-child limit'. There is more information about this in Chapter 2.

Some non-looked-after children in kinship care are exempt from the two-child limit. You can get amounts included for them in your universal credit or child tax credit, if one of the following applies:

- the child is living with you as a result of a child arrangements order under section 8 of the Children Act 1989
- you have been appointed as a special guardian for the child under section 14A of the Children Act 1989
- you are entitled to guardian's allowance for the child
- you have a kinship care order under section 11 of the Children (Scotland) Act 1995
- you have been appointed as a guardian for the child under section 5 of the Children Act 1989 or section 7 of the Children (Scotland) Act 1995
- one of the above bullet points applied to you before the child's 16th birthday and you have continued to be responsible for her/him since then
- you have taken on the care of the child where it is likely that otherwise s/he would have been looked after by the local authority

This means that even if you already have two or more dependent children and you start caring for a child (or children) in one of these circumstances, you can get the child element in your universal credit or child tax credit for that child. If you give birth to a child after taking on the care of a child or children in one of these circumstances, the child or children in a kinship care arrangement is 'disregarded' when applying the two-child limit.

Does someone else also want to claim benefits for the same child?

The main benefits that you may want to claim to cover the additional costs of looking after a child are child benefit and the 'child element' of universal credit. A child can only be included in one person's benefit award.

To get child benefit, you must be responsible for the child. This usually means that the child lives with you. 'Living with' means that the child lives in the same house or residence and has a settled course of daily living there. If there are competing claims for child benefit, the person with whom the child normally lives has priority.

However, if someone else is getting child benefit for the child when you make a claim, the other person usually keeps the child benefit for three weeks after you make your claim – this means you do not usually become entitled to child benefit until three weeks after the week in which you claim.

You should get the child element in universal credit if the child 'normally lives' with you. You do not have to be getting child benefit for her/him. If a child comes to live with you full time and the arrangement is reasonably settled, it is very likely that the child will be treated as normally living with you. This means that if someone else has been getting universal credit for the child, her/his payments stop. Similar rules apply for child tax credit, although you will usually only be able to get child tax credit for the child if you are already getting tax credits.

You are treated as responsible for a child for income support and jobseeker's allowance if either of the following applies:

- you get child benefit for the child
- no one gets child benefit for the child, and s/he usually lives with you or you are the only person who has claimed child benefit for her/him

This may be important if, for example, you want to get income support on the basis of being a lone parent.

You are treated as responsible for a child for housing benefit purposes if s/he is 'normally living' with you. This means that s/he spends more time in your household than in any other. If it is unclear in whose household the child normally lives, or if s/he spends equal time in more than one household, you are treated as having responsibility if one of the following applies:

- you get child benefit for the child
- no one gets child benefit, but you have claimed it
- no one has claimed child benefit, or more than one person has claimed it, but you appear to have most responsibility for the child

If the child has a disability and gets disability living allowance, you can apply to become her/his 'appointee'. The appointee receives the disability living allowance on behalf of the child. If you believe that the child should be getting disability living allowance, you can make the claim.

If you are caring for a child with a disability and someone else is also providing care for her/him, you must agree between yourselves who should claim carer's allowance. If you cannot agree, the Department for Work and Pensions decides.

Is there a delay in getting your benefit paid?
If you experience delays in getting your benefits and tax credits sorted out, you may be able to get some financial help from your children's services or social work department to help you continue to care for the child. It is also possible to get an 'interim payment' or an 'advance' of some benefits, if there is a delay with your claim. There is more information about delays and what help you may be able to get in Chapter 10.

Chapter 10
Dealing with problems

This chapter covers:

1. What help is available?

2. Are you waiting for your benefit?

3. Has your benefit been reduced by the benefit cap?

4. Has your universal credit reduced because of how your wages are paid?

5. Has your benefit been reduced by a sanction?

6. Do you disagree with a decision?

7. Have you been overpaid?

8. What other help is there in an emergency?

What you need to know

- You may be able to get a benefit advance while you are waiting for your benefit to be paid.

- If your benefit is reduced because of the 'benefit cap', you may be eligible for a discretionary housing payment.

- Your universal credit may be reduced depending on when your wages are paid.

- Most decisions, including the decision to 'sanction' your benefit, can be challenged.

- If you are overpaid, you may be able to challenge the decision, or ask for the overpayment to be written off or reduced.

- In an emergency, you may be able to get a local welfare payment, or help from food banks or the local authority.

1. What help is available?

In the benefits system, things often cause hardship or go wrong. When that happens, there are various solutions, depending on what has happened. This chapter describes common situations where people find themselves without money, or are otherwise unhappy with their benefit claim, and potential ways to address these problems.

> Box A
> **Financial help in an emergency: checklist**
> * short-term benefit advance
> * discretionary housing payments
> * hardship payments
> * compensation payments
> * local welfare assistance
> * Children Act payments
> * food banks and charities

2. Are you waiting for your benefit?

If you are waiting for a decision on your universal credit or you are waiting for your first payment, you may be able to get a universal credit 'advance'. You can get up to 100 per cent of your estimated award paid within five days of requesting an advance, although it is often paid more quickly than this.

To get an advance, you must be in financial need. This means there is a risk to the health and safety of you, your partner or your child(ren) if you are not paid an advance. If you have transferred from any of the benefits or tax credits that universal credit replaces in the last month, you are treated as being in financial need.

You must repay the advance out of your universal credit award, which can mean a reduction in your payments for up to 12 months, but you are not charged interest on the advance. You can also get a universal credit advance at other times – eg, if you are waiting for an increased payment because your circumstances have changed and you should now be paid more universal credit.

You can get a 'short-term advance' for jobseeker's allowance and employment and support allowance and some other benefits. There are no advance payments of child benefit, but you can apply for an 'interim payment'.

The Department for Work and Pensions encourages you to apply for a universal credit advance using your online account. You can also apply for an advance payment at your initial interview or by phoning the universal credit helpline on 0800 328 5644. For other benefits, you can request a short-term advance at the job centre or use the telephone number for the specific benefit at gov.uk/short-term-benefit-advance.

3. Has your benefit been reduced by the benefit cap?

The total amount of benefit you can be paid may be limited by a 'benefit cap'. If you are affected, the amount of your housing benefit or universal credit is reduced.

If you have a child and are getting housing benefit, the benefit cap is £384.62 a week, or £442.31 a week if you live in Greater London. If you are getting universal credit, it is £1,666.67 a month, or £1,916.67 a month if you live in Greater London.

The cap is calculated by adding together the total amount of all the benefits you receive, including child benefit. Some benefits are not included – eg, bereavement support payment.

In some situations, you are exempt from having the cap applied. These include if:

- you, your partner or any of your children get disability living allowance or personal independence payment
- you or your partner get carer's allowance
- you or your partner are working and your earnings are over a certain amount or you get working tax credit

If you have been working and earning over a certain amount over the last year, your universal credit will not be reduced by the benefit cap for nine months after you stop work. To make sure this 'grace period' is applied to your universal credit, have details ready of your earnings for the last year when you claim.

EXAMPLE

The benefit cap

David and Marie have three children. Their monthly income from benefits is universal credit of £1,946.95 and child benefit of £212.12. This is a total of £2,159.07 a month. The benefit cap means they can only get a maximum of £1,666.67 a month from benefits. Their universal credit is therefore reduced by £492.40 a month. They apply to their local authority for a discretionary housing payment to help with the cost of their rent.

If you are affected by the benefit cap, you should apply for a discretionary housing payment. There is more information about these in Chapter 6.

What families say

Benefit cap

'A family with three children have had their benefits cut because they are affected by the benefit cap. They live in a rural location, so the costs of basics, including heating and food, are already more expensive. They run a car to allow the family to get about. The family are quite isolated in the area and the house is very poor. The children attend clubs to give them a social life and make friends. The cost of the benefit cap means that the children either need to stop attending the clubs or the rent will not get paid.' *Housing association welfare rights officer*

4. Has your universal credit reduced because of how your wages are paid?

Universal credit is calculated over a monthly 'assessment period'. Wages are taken into account in the assessment period in which they are paid. If you are paid two lots of monthly wages in one assessment period, perhaps because wages are paid early, they can be allocated over two assessment periods to avoid your universal credit payments changing. However, if you are paid weekly, fortnightly or four weekly, your regular pay is not reallocated when an extra payday falls in an assessment period. Your universal credit will reduce or end in these months. If universal credit ends, reclaim the following month. Your assessment period and universal credit payment day will stay the same. You may also be able to challenge the decision to end or reduce your award, depending on your circumstances.

EXAMPLES

Universal credit and earning patterns

Carmen's wages are normally paid on the 25th of the month but, because of the May bank holiday, she is paid early on the 22nd May. Both her 25 April and 22 May wages fall in the same universal credit assessment period. The Department for Work and Pensions allocates her May wages to the next assessment period and there is no change to her universal credit.

Graeme's wages are paid four-weekly. He usually gets a universal credit payment of £300 each month. In his February assessment period he receives two sets of wages, meaning his earnings in this assessment period are too high for him to get any universal credit. The award ends and he gets no universal credit payment for February. He then reclaims universal credit and is paid his normal payment of £300 next month.

5. Has your benefit been reduced by a sanction?

If you do not fulfil your work-related responsibilities, you may have a 'sanction' applied to your universal credit, jobseeker's allowance, income support or employment and support allowance. This means your benefit is paid at a reduced rate, and might even be reduced to nil. This can happen if, for example, you fail to attend a 'work-focused interview' or if you are found not to be actively looking for work. The sanctions can be severe, so you should always try to avoid one if you can.

What should you do?

A 'sanction' should not be applied if you have a good reason for your actions. All your circumstances should be taken into account when deciding whether you had a good reason for not complying with something – including if you were ill, or if your disability, caring responsibilities, language or transport problems meant you could not attend an interview or undertake an activity.

If you are given a sanction, you can challenge the decision – first by asking for a 'mandatory reconsideration' of the decision and then by appealing to an independent tribunal.

EXAMPLE

Challenging a sanction: good reason

Chloe is a lone parent with a two year old child. She gets universal credit. She is told that she must attend a skills assessment course, but on the day of the course her child is ill and she cannot go. She informs the Department for Work and Pensions, but the following week her universal credit is reduced because of a sanction. She asks the Department for Work and Pensions to look at the decision again. She tells it that she had a good reason for not attending and provides evidence of a visit to the doctor with her child. The decision is overturned and her universal credit is paid in full from when it was reduced.

If your universal credit is sanctioned, you may be able to apply for a hardship payment. Hardship payments are not made automatically, you must apply for one. You must have met all your 'work-related requirements' in the week before you apply and the Department for Work and Pensions must accept that you cannot meet your basic needs for rent, heating, food and hygiene. You should try to get help from other sources such as family and friends first, but you are not exepcted to get into debt on a credit card or bank loan. Hardship payments cover one assessment period, which means you will need to reapply each month. The best way to make sure you receive a hardship payment is to reapply for one every universal credit pay day that your usual payment is reduced. Hardship payments are repaid from your universal credit award, which means future payments will be reduced. You can apply for a hardship payment by phoning the universal credit helpline on 0800 328 5644.

What CPAG says

Challenging a sanction

- Should the requirement have been applied to you in the first place? For example, does your claimant commitment record that, in fact, you were able to limit your activity in the way that you did?

- Were you properly informed of the requirement and what would happen if you failed to comply with it? If not, the sanction may not be lawful.

- Did you, in fact, fail to carry out the requirement? For example, if you turned up for an appointment just a few minutes late, you may be able to argue that this does not mean you failed to comply. If you have to look for work, did you carry out all such activity as could reasonably be expected of you?

- Did you have a good reason for your actions? 'Good reason' is not defined in the law and all the circumstances should be taken into account, including your health, a domestic emergency, transport difficulties, domestic violence or bullying, language and literacy problems, and sincerely held religious or conscientious objections.

If your jobseeker's allowance is sanctioned, you can apply for a hardship payment. First check whether the jobseeker's allowance you get is called 'new-style' jobseeker's allowance. If it is, then you need to apply for a universal credit hardship payment. If your jobseeker's allowance is 'income-based', you can apply for a hardship payment of jobseeker's allowance which you do not need to pay back.

6. Do you disagree with a decision?

Can you appeal?

If you disagree with a decision about your benefit, you may be able to challenge it. You can challenge most decisions about benefits and tax credits by appealing to an independent tribunal.

Before you can appeal, you must ask for the decision to be looked at again (except if it is about your housing benefit). This is called a 'mandatory reconsideration'. If you want to challenge a housing benefit decision, you can appeal without first having to ask for a mandatory reconsideration.

You must usually ask for a mandatory reconsideration within one month of the date the decision was sent to you, or 30 days for tax credits. If it has been longer than a month, you can still get a decision looked at again if there are special reasons to extend the time limit (for up to one year maximum). You may also be able to get the decision looked at again if there are particular grounds for doing so – eg, if the person making the decision about your benefit made a mistake.

If you are late asking for a mandatory reconsideration, and it is not accepted that the time limit should be extended, you can still appeal, provided it is within 13 months of the original decision.

If you are still unhappy with the decision following a mandatory reconsideration, you can appeal to an independent tribunal. You must do so within one month of the date of the mandatory reconsideration decision, or within 30 days for tax credits. This time limit can be extended by one year from the usual time limit, if there are special reasons for doing so.

You must appeal in writing, preferably using the appropriate appeal form. For housing benefit, use the form provided by your local authority. For tax credits and child benefit, use Form SSCS5. For other benefits, use Form SSCS1, which is available from gov.uk/government/collections/court-and-tribunal-forms.

In Scotland, the Best Start grant, funeral support payment and Scottish child payment are administered by Social Security Scotland. If you disagree with a decision (referred to as a 'determination' by Social Security Scotland) about these benefits, you can request a 'redetermination'. To request a redetermination from Social Security Scotland you can complete the form sent with the determination or you can call the helpline on 0800 182 2222. You must usually request a redetermination within 31 days of the date you were notified of the determination. This can be extended by a year if you have a good reason for not requesting a redetermination sooner. If you disagree with the redetermination, you can appeal to an independent tribunal.

EXAMPLE

Appealing

Greg splits up with his partner and moves into his mother's house with his two children. He claims universal credit as a single parent. His claim is refused because the Department for Work and Pensions thinks he still lives with his partner. He requests a mandatory reconsideration of the decision, but the decision is not changed. He then appeals to an independent tribunal. The tribunal accepts that he is single and he is awarded universal credit from the date he first claimed it.

Can you complain?

If you are unhappy with the way your claim has been handled, or you experience delays in getting your benefit or tax credits claim decided, you could use the Department for Work and Pensions, HM Revenue and Customs or local authority complaints procedure. In the first instance, you should take up the issue with the office dealing with it. Contact details should be on any letters you have about your claim. You should follow the relevant complaints procedure.

Once you have gone through all the steps in the complaints procedure, if you are still unhappy with the response, you can take your case to the Independent Case Examiner (Department for Work and Pensions benefits), the Adjudicator (tax credits) or Ombudsman for local authorities.

If you are still not happy, you can contact your MP about the matter and ask her/him to refer your complaint to the Parliamentary and Health Service Ombudsman.

You can ask for compensation if you are dissatisfied with the way your claim has been administered. You may be able to get compensation from the Department for Work and Pensions, HM Revenue and Customs or the local authority if you can show that you have lost out or suffered through their error or delay.

In Scotland, if you want to complain about the way you have been treated by Social Security Scotland, you can call the helpline on 0800 182 2222. If you are still unhappy after Social Security Scotland has dealt with your complaint, you can contact the Scottish Public Services Ombudsman.

7. Have you been overpaid?

If more benefit is paid to you than you are entitled to, you have been overpaid.

There are many reasons why benefits are overpaid – eg, if you gave the wrong information when you claimed, you are late reporting a change in your circumstances, or the relevant department does not act on the information you give.

If you are overpaid, you may be asked to repay the overpayment. You should check your award carefully. If you disagree that you have been overpaid or with the amount you have been overpaid, you can challenge the decision.

Even if you agree that you have been overpaid, you may be able to challenge the decision. You only have to repay an overpayment of most benefits if it was caused by your giving incorrect information, or because you failed to tell the benefit authorities of a relevant change in your circumstances. Housing benefit and benefits paid by Social Security Scotland (Best Start grant, funeral support payment and

Scottish child payment) have slightly different rules, and you may have to repay an overpayment even if you gave correct information, if you could have realised you were being overpaid. However, for tax credits, universal credit and other benefits under the universal credit system, in most cases you will have to repay an overpayment even if you gave all the correct information and reported any changes.

Even if you are asked to repay an overpayment, you can ask for some or all of the overpayment to be written off. However, this is at the authority's discretion.

8. What other help is there in an emergency?

Can you get a local welfare payment?

You may be able to get help from your local authority under its local welfare assistance scheme. In England, each local authority has its own scheme. In Wales and Scotland, the Discretionary Assistance Fund for Wales and the Scottish Welfare Fund are administered by your local authority.

You may be able to get help if you are in one of the following situations.

- You need help with an immediate short-term need in a crisis – eg, if you do not have sufficient resources, or you need help with expenses in an emergency or as a result of a disaster, such as a fire or flood in your home.

- You need to establish yourself in the community following a stay in institutional or residential accommodation, or to help you remain in the community.

- You need help to set up a home in the community as part of a planned resettlement programme.

- You need help to ease exceptional pressure on your family.

- You need help to enable you to care for a prisoner or young offender on temporary release.

- You need help with certain travel expenses – eg, to visit someone in hospital, to attend a funeral, to ease a domestic crisis, to visit a child living with her/his other parent or to move to suitable accommodation.

> **EXAMPLE**
>
> **Help to ease exceptional pressure on your family**
>
> May is a lone parent with three children. She has been rehoused following domestic violence, and needs beds for the children, a cooker and a sofa. She applies to the local welfare assistance scheme and gets a community care grant to buy these items.

In England, the local scheme is entirely at your local authority's discretion. Check with your local authority to find out what help is available, whether you qualify and how to apply.

In Wales, the Discretionary Assistance Fund for Wales offers non-repayable emergency assistance payments and individual assistance payments. Find out how to apply at gov.wales/discretionary-assistance-fund-daf/how-apply.

In Scotland, the Scottish Welfare Fund provides community care grants and crisis grants. The basic rules for the scheme are set by the Scottish government, with each local authority having some discretion. You should apply to your local authority.

Can you get any other help from your local authority?

In England and Wales, local authorities have a duty under section 17 of the Children Act 1989 to provide services to children who are in need.

In Scotland, the local authority social work department has powers under section 22 of the Children (Scotland) Act 1995 and under section 12 of the Social Work (Scotland) Act 1968 allowing it to assist people in need.

In all these cases, assistance can be provided in cash or in kind – eg, vouchers to buy food. However, your local authority may refer you to a local food bank rather than providing you with any direct help.

Can you use a food bank?

You may be able to get help from a food bank if there is one in your area. Food banks can provide essential food and household items free of charge to people in need. Some food banks operate under the umbrella organisation called The Trussell Trust; others are independent. Food banks are often run from local churches or community centres. You may have to be referred to the food bank by an agency, such as a social worker, GP practice or Citizens Advice.

Can you get help from a charity?

You may be able to get some assistance from a charity, although this may be more likely to help with specific items (eg, furniture) than provide immediate financial help. Which charity to approach can depend on your personal circumstances, such as having a particular health problem or having worked in a particular job.

Further information

See CPAG's *Welfare Benefits and Tax Credits Handbook* for more detailed information on benefits and tax credits.

You can find your nearest Trussell Trust food bank at trusselltrust.org.

Search for charitable grants that may be able to help you at grants-search.turn2us.org.uk.

Chapter 11
A to Z of benefits

Attendance allowance

Attendance allowance is a benefit paid by the Department for Work and Pensions to people who have care needs as a result of their disability and who are 'pension age' or over when they claim. It is not affected by your income or capital, and you do not have to have paid national insurance contributions.

Who can claim?

You qualify if all of the following apply.

- You have reached 'pension age'.
- You satisfy conditions about residence and presence in the UK and you are not a 'person subject to immigration control'.
- You satisfy a disability test. This tests whether you need help with your 'bodily functions', or whether you require supervision to avoid substantial danger to yourself or others. Depending on the amount of help you need, you may qualify for a lower or higher rate.

How much do you get?

Lower rate: £59.70 a week.

Higher rate: £89.15 a week.

How do you claim?

Claim on Form AA1, available from the Department for Work and Pensions Attendance Allowance helpline on 0800 731 0122 (Relay UK dial 18001 first; textphone 0800 731 0317). Requesting a form on the helpline is the best way to secure the earliest date for your claim, but you can also download a claim form from gov.uk/attendance-allowance/how-to-claim.

Bereavement benefits

Bereavement benefits are benefits paid by the Department for Work and Pensions to widows, widowers or surviving civil partners. They are not affected by your income or capital. Your late spouse or civil partner must have satisfied certain national insurance contribution conditions, or died as the result of an industrial accident or disease.

If your spouse or civil partner died on or after 6 April 2017, you may be able to claim **bereavement support payment**. If s/he died before 6 April 2017, you may be able to get one of the previous bereavement benefits: a lump-sum **bereavement payment, widowed parent's allowance,** if you have children or are pregnant, and **bereavement allowance,** if you were at least 45 when s/he died.

Unmarried partners have not been able to claim bereavement benefits. There are plans to change the rules so that if you have children and your partner has died, you will be able to claim bereavement support payment or widowed parent's allowance if you and your late partner were not married or civil partners.

Who can claim?

You qualify for **bereavement support payment** if all of the following apply.

- You are under 'pension age'.
- Your spouse or civil partner died on or after 6 April 2017 (to be entitled for the maximum 18-month period, you must claim within

three months of the death; to be entitled at all, you must claim within 21 months of the death).

- Your spouse or civil partner had either paid sufficient national insurance contributions or was employed and died as the result of an industrial injury or disease.
- You meet certain residence conditions.

It is paid for a maximum of 18 months.

You qualify for **widowed parent's allowance** if all of the following apply.

- You are under 'pension age'.
- You have not remarried, entered into a civil partnership or started living with another person as if you were married or in a civil partnership.
- Your spouse or civil partner died before 6 April 2017.
- Your spouse or civil partner either had a sufficient national insurance record or was employed and died as the result of an industrial accident or disease.
- You are entitled to child benefit for a child and your late partner was her/his parent.

How much do you get?

Bereavement support payment

Initial lump sum: £2,500 standard rate; £3,500 higher rate.

Monthly amount: £100 standard rate; £350 higher rate.

You get the higher rate if you had children or were pregnant when your spouse or civil partner died.

Widowed parent's allowance

£121.95 a week. The rate is reduced if your late spouse/civil partner had an incomplete national insurance record.

How do you claim?

Claim by phoning the Department for Work and Pensions Bereavement Service on 0800 731 0469 (Relay UK dial 18001 first; textphone 0800 731 0464).

Alternatively, you can use a claim form. For bereavement support payment, use Form BSP1, available from gov.uk/bereavement-support-payment/how-to-claim. For widowed parent's allowance, use Form BB1, available from gov.uk/widowed-parents-allowance/how-to-claim. Both are also available by phoning Jobcentre Plus on 0800 055 6688 (textphone 0800 023 4888).

Best Start grant

The Best Start grant is made up of three one-off payments to help with the costs of having a child in the family. It is only available in Scotland and is paid by Social Security Scotland. If you are in England or Wales, see the information on Sure Start maternity grants on page 187.

To qualify for a Best Start grant you must meet the following basic rules.

- You are ordinarily resident in Scotland.
- Unless you are under 18 (or in some situations under 20), you or your partner are getting one or more of the following 'qualifying benefits':
  - universal credit (including if your award ended within the last month)
  - income support
  - income-based jobseeker's allowance
  - income-related employment and support allowance
  - pension credit
  - housing benefit
  - child tax credit
  - working tax credit
- You meet the conditions for the pregancy and baby payment, the early learning payment or the school-age payment.

Who can claim a pregnancy and baby payment?

This is a grant to help with the costs of having a new baby.

You must satisfy the basic rules for a Best Start grant. You can qualify from the 24th week of pregnancy up to six months after the baby is born (including if the baby is stillborn or dies within this period).

You may also qualify if you become responsible for a baby who is under the age of one – eg, as a 'kinship carer' or where a child is placed with you for adoption. You have to claim before the child's first birthday.

Box A
Are you responsible for a child?

You are responsible for a child for the Best Start grant if any of the following applies on the day you claim.

- The child is your dependant. S/he counts as your dependant if you get child benefit for her/him or s/he is included in your universal credit, child tax credit or pension credit award.

- You are under 20, the parent of the child, you normally live with her/him and you are a dependant in someone else's child benefit, universal credit, child tax credit or pension credit.

- You have adopted the child under Scottish law, or under the law of another jurisdiction recognised under Scottish law.

- The child has been placed with you for adoption and you are then appointed as her/his guardian.

- You are a 'kinship carer' and the child lives with you under a kinship care order or an agreement with a local authority.

- You have a parental order following a surrogate pregnancy.

Who can claim an early learning payment?

This is a grant to help with the costs of having a young child aged between two and three and a half.

You must satisfy the basic rules for a Best Start grant and you must be responsible for the child (Box A). You must claim between the child's second birthday and the date six months after her/his third birthday.

Who can claim a school-age payment?

This is a grant to help with the costs of a child reaching school age.

You must satisfy the basic rules for a Best Start grant and be responsible for the child (Box A).

If your child's date of birth falls between 1 March 2015 and 29 February 2016 (inclusive), you have to claim between 1 June 2020 and 28 February 2021. If your child's date of birth falls between 1 March 2016 and 28 February 2017 (inclusive), you have to claim between 1 June 2021 and 28 February 2022. These time limits can be extended if they are not met due to the coronavirus pandemic.

How much do you get?

Pregnancy and baby payment: £600 (or £300 if you already have a child).

Early learning payment: £250.

School-age payment: £250.

How do you claim?

Claim at mygov.scot/best-start-grant or by phoning 0800 182 2222.

Carer's allowance

Carer's allowance is a benefit paid by the Department for Work and Pensions to people who spend at least 35 hours a week looking after a disabled adult or disabled child. Temporary breaks in caring are allowed in certain circumstances. If you are working, you must not be earning more than £128 a week. Otherwise, it is not affected by your income or capital, and you do not have to have paid national insurance contributions.

Who can claim?

You qualify if all of the following apply.

- You are aged at least 16.
- You are caring for a person who is receiving:
  - attendance allowance
  - either the highest or the middle rate of disability living allowance care component
  - either rate of the daily living component of personal independence payment
  - armed forces independence payment
  - constant attendance allowance with an industrial injury benefit or war pension.
- You are providing care for at least 35 hours a week.
- You are not earning more than £128 a week.
- You are not a full-time student.
- You satisfy certain residence conditions and you are not a 'person subject to immigration control'.

How much do you get?

£67.20 a week.

If you live in Scotland and get carer's allowance, you are also entitled to a carer's allowance supplement. This is usually paid twice a year as a lump sum payment. In 2020/21, the payments were £230.10 each. You must be resident in Scotland and getting carer's allowance on a qualifying date. The supplement does not affect your other benefits.

How do you claim?

Claim online or download Form DS700 (DS700(SP) if you get a state pension) from gov.uk/carers-allowance/how-to-claim. You can also claim by phoning the Carer's Allowance Unit on 0800 731 0317 (Relay

UK dial 18001 first; textphone 0800 731 0297 5312), or by phoning your local Jobcentre Plus office.

Child benefit

Child benefit is a benefit paid by HM Revenue and Customs to people who are responsible for a child. It is paid for each child for whom you are responsible, with a higher amount paid for the eldest child. You do not have to be the child's parent. Child benefit is not affected by your income or capital, and you do not have to have paid national insurance contributions. If you or your partner have an annual income of over £50,000, you may pay additional income tax to recover the child benefit.

Who can claim?

You qualify if all of the following apply.

- The child counts as either a 'child' or a 'qualifying young person'. This includes all children under 16, and those aged between 16 and 19 in 'non-advanced education' at school or college (eg, studying GCSEs, AS and A levels, NVQ level 3 or below, Scottish National Qualifications up to Higher or Advanced Higher level or for a BTEC) for more than 12 hours a week, or those aged between 16 and 19 in approved training.
- You are responsible for the child. The child must live with you, or you must contribute at least the rate of child benefit to the cost of supporting her/him.
- You have priority over anyone else. If someone else tries to claim child benefit, you have priority if the child lives with you, if you are the wife and you are living with your husband, or you are the child's mother and you are not married to your partner.
- You and the child satisfy certain presence and residence conditions, and you are not a 'person subject to immigration control'.
- The child is not getting universal credit, income support, income-based jobseeker's allowance, employment and support allowance or tax credits in her/his own right.

In certain circumstances, you cannot get child benefit, including if the child is being looked after by a local authority, is living as part of a couple, or is in prison or other custody.

How much do you get?

Only or eldest child: £21.05 a week.

Other child(ren): £13.95 a week.

How do you claim?

Claim on Form CH2, available from gov.uk/government/publications/child-benefit-claim-form-ch2 or from the HM Revenue and Customs Child Benefit Office on 0300 200 3100 (Relay UK dial 18001 first; textphone 0300 200 3103).

Council tax reduction

Council tax reduction is help with council tax for people on a low income. It reduces the amount of council tax you have to pay – it is not a payment of money. The reduction in your council tax is made by your local authority.

Who can claim?

You qualify if all of the following apply.

- You or your partner are liable for council tax for the home in which you live.
- You satisfy the 'habitual residence test' and the 'right to reside test' and you are not a 'person subject to immigration control'.
- Your savings are under £16,000 (unless you get the 'guarantee credit' of pension credit).
- Your income is sufficiently low.

How much is the reduction?

The amount of council tax reduction you get depends on your circumstances. In England and Wales, local authorities may have their own way of calculating what help you can get. In Scotland, there is a national scheme applied by all local authorities. In all the schemes, the local authority take into account things like your household income and how many other adults and children live with you.

How do you claim?

Claim from your local authority. An official site with a postcode finder for contacting your local authority about council tax reduction is at gov.uk/apply-council-tax-reduction.

Disability living allowance

Disability living allowance is a benefit paid by the Department for Work and Pensions to people who have care needs and/or mobility problems because of a disability. It is not affected by your income or capital, and you do not have to have paid national insurance contributions.

New claims can now only be made for children under 16. Disability living allowance for adults is being replaced by personal independence payment. If you are already getting disability living allowance and are under 65 years old, at some point you will have your award reassessed to see whether you qualify for personal independence payment.

Who can claim?

You qualify if all of the following apply:

- You are aged under 16 when you first claim.
- You meet certain conditions about residence and presence in the UK and you are not a 'person subject to immigration control'.

- You satisfy a disability test:
  - If you need help with your care needs, the disability test looks at whether you need help with your 'bodily functions', or whether you require supervision to avoid substantial danger to yourself or others. Depending on the amount of help you need, you may qualify for one of three rates.
  - If you need help with mobility problems, the test looks at whether you are 'virtually unable to walk' or have certain severe disabilities (for the higher rate), or whether you need guidance or supervision to walk (for the lower rate). A child must be at least three years old to get the higher rate of the mobility component and at least five to get the lower rate.

A child must need substantially more help than a child of the same age without a disability would need.

How much do you get?

Care component

Lowest rate: £23.60 a week.

Middle rate: £59.70 a week.

Highest rate: £89.15 a week.

Mobility component

Lower rate: £23.60 a week.

Higher rate: £62.25 a week.

How do you claim?

Claim on Form DLA1A Child, available from the Department for Work and Pensions Disability Living Allowance helpline on 0800 121 4600 (Relay UK dial 18001 first; textphone 0800 121 4523) (it is best to request the form from the helpline as, if you complete and return it within six weeks, the claim is dated from the date of your call) or from gov.uk/government/publications/disability-living-allowance-for-children-claim-form.

Discretionary housing payments

Discretionary housing payments are discretionary payments that your local authority can make to people who are entitled to housing benefit or help with their rent in their universal credit, but who need additional financial help to cover their housing costs.

The local authority has discretion whether or not to pay you, how much to pay you and over what period.

Employment and support allowance

Employment and support allowance is a benefit paid by the Department for Work and Pensions to people who cannot work because of illness or disability. This is known as having 'limited capability for work' and the Department for Work and Pensions assesses it using a test called the 'work capability assessment'.

There are two types of employment and support allowance: income-related and contributory. You can be entitled to both. However, income-related employment and support allowance is being replaced by universal credit and in most cases you cannot make a new claim for it.

Income-related employment and support allowance

Income-related employment and support allowance is for people unable to work and who are on a low income. Your entitlement is affected by your income and capital, but you do not need to have paid national insurance contributions.

Income-related employment and support allowance is being replaced by universal credit. If you come under the universal credit system, you cannot make a new claim for income-related employment and support allowance. At some point, people already getting income-related employment and support allowance will be transferred to universal credit.

Who can claim?

Usually you can only make a new claim for income-related employment and support allowance if you (or your current partner) are getting or have recently been getting an extra amount for severe disability (a 'severe disability premium') in another 'means-tested benefit'. This rule is currently due to end on 27 January 2021. Otherwise, if you make a new claim for any kind of employment and support allowance, you cannot get income-related employment and support allowance.

You qualify for income-related employment and support allowance if all of the following apply.

- You do not come under the universal credit system.
- You have 'limited capability for work'.
- You are aged at least 16 and under 'pension age'.
- You are not getting income support, jobseeker's allowance, pension credit or statutory sick pay.
- Your partner is not getting income support, income-based jobseeker's allowance, pension credit or income-related employment and support allowance.
- You are not working (although certain work is permitted).
- You are not in full-time education (but disabled students may qualify).
- You do not have more than £16,000 in capital and your income is sufficiently low.
- You are in Great Britain, satisfy the 'habitual residence test' and the 'right to reside test' and you are not a 'person subject to immigration control'.

How much do you get?

The Department for Work and Pensions calculates your entitlement. In the calculation, basic amounts are included for you and your partner. Amounts for children are not included. After an initial assessment phase, an additional amount (known as a 'support component') of £39.20 is then included if you are assessed as being so ill that you are not required to undertake any 'work-related activity'. The Department for Work of Pensions calls this the 'support group'. Before 3 April 2017, claimants who were assessed as not being in the support group got an additional amount (a 'work-related activity component') of £29.55 included. If you were entitled to this component, you can continue to get it.

The actual amount you get depends on your circumstances – including whether you have a severe disability or you are a carer, and the amount of your income and capital. The circumstances (including any income and capital) of your partner are also taken into account. The Department for Work and Pensions provides links to independent benefit calculators at gov.uk/benefits-calculators.

How do you claim?

Claim income-related employment and support allowance by phoning a Jobcentre Plus contact centre on 0800 169 0350 (Relay UK dial 18001 first; textphone 0800 023 4888). You may then be asked to download an ESA1 form from gov.uk/government/publications/employment-and-support-allowance-claim-form.

If you are already getting contributory employment and support allowance, you may not need to make a new claim for income-related employment and support allowance.

Contributory employment and support allowance

Contributory employment and support allowance is for people unable to work who have paid sufficient national insurance contributions to qualify. It is not affected by your income and capital.

Contributory employment and support allowance is not being replaced by universal credit. You can get it at the same time as getting universal credit, in which case the Department for Work and Pensions calls it 'new-style' employment and support allowance. If you do not come under the universal credit system, you can get it topped up with income-related employment and support allowance instead, in which case the Department for Work and Pensions calls it 'old-style' contributory employment and support allowance. If you are getting 'old-style' contributory employment and support allowance, you can get it topped up with income-related employment and support allowance without having to make a new claim – your current award can be adjusted to include the income-related form.

Who can claim?
You qualify if all of the following apply.

- You have 'limited capability for work'.
- You are aged at least 16 and under 'pension age'.
- You are in Great Britain.
- You are not getting income support, jobseeker's allowance or statutory sick pay.
- You satisfy certain national insurance contribution conditions, including having paid sufficient class 1 or class 2 contributions in one of the last two recent tax years before the year of your claim – so you must have been working at least at some point in those years.
- You are not working (although certain work is permitted).

How much do you get?
You get an amount for yourself. Amounts for your partner and children are not included. There is a basic amount during an initial assessment phase (usually 13 weeks) of £58.90 if you are aged under 25, or £74.35 if you are aged 25 or over. After the assessment phase, the basic amount is £74.35 in all cases. An additional 'support component' of £39.20 is then included if you are assessed as being so ill that you are not required to undertake any 'work-related activity'. The Department for Work and Pensions calls this the 'support group'. Before 3 April 2017, claimants who were assessed as not being in the support group got an additional amount (a 'work-related activity component') of £29.55 included. If you were entitled to this component, you can continue to get it.

How do you claim?
Claim 'new-style' contributory employment and support allowance at gov.uk/guidance/new-style-employment-and-support-allowance. If you cannot claim online, phone 0800 328 5644 (Relay UK dial 18001 first; textphone 0800 328 1344).

If you do not come under the universal credit system, you can claim 'old-style' contributory employment and support allowance in the same way as you would claim income-related employment and support allowance.

Funeral support payment

A funeral support payment is made to help with burial or cremation costs. It is only available in Scotland and is paid by Social Security Scotland. If you are in England or Wales, see the information about funeral expenses payment on page 188.

Who can claim?

You qualify if all of the following apply.

- You live in Scotland.
- You or your partner get one or more of the following qualifying benefits:
  - universal credit (including if your award ended in the last month)
  - income support
  - income-based jobseeker's allowance
  - income-related employment and support allowance
  - child tax credit
  - working tax credit including the disabled worker or severe disability element
  - pension credit
  - housing benefit
- You or your partner have accepted responsibility for the funeral costs and it is reasonable for you to have done so. Usually, it will be reasonable for the person with the closest relationship to the person who has died to accept responsibility, but other factors, such as estrangement, may also be relevant.
- The person who has died was ordinarily resident in the UK.
- The funeral takes place in the UK (but a funeral in a European Economic Area state may sometimes qualify).
- You claim within six months of the funeral.

How much do you get?

The funeral support payment covers the cost of a burial plot, necessary burial fees and cremation fees. It also covers the costs of any medical certificates required and any documentation required for the release of the assets of the person who has died. Some other funeral expenses may also be covered.

How do you claim?

Claim at mygov.scot/funeral-support-payment, by phoning 0800 182 2222 or on a claim form which you can download online or request on the phone.

Guardian's allowance

Guardian's allowance is a benefit paid by HM Revenue and Customs to people looking after a child who is, in effect, an orphan. Your entitlement is not affected by your income or capital, and you do not have to have paid national insurance contributions.

Who can claim?

You qualify if the following apply.

- You are entitled to child benefit for the child.
- The child is an orphan, or one of her/his parents has died and all reasonable efforts to trace the other parent have been unsuccessful, or s/he is in prison or detained in hospital.

How much do you get?

£17.90 a week.

How do you claim?

Claim on Form BG1, available from the HM Revenue and Customs Guardian's Allowance Unit on 0300 322 9080 (textphone 0300 200

3103) or from gov.uk/government/publications/guardians-allowance-claim-form-bg1.

Health benefits

Health benefits can provide help with the costs of NHS prescriptions, dental treatment, sight tests and glasses, wigs and fabric supports, as well as fares to receive NHS treatment. Health benefits help by providing such items free or at a reduced cost – they are not payments of money. Health benefits are awarded by the NHS Business Services Authority.

Who can claim?

You qualify if you are in an exempt group, so you get the item free of charge. You are in an exempt group if you or a member of your family gets income support, income-based jobseeker's allowance, income-related employment and support allowance, the 'guarantee credit' of pension credit or, depending on your income, universal credit or tax credits. Other people in exempt groups include young people in education, pregnant women and asylum seekers.

Alternatively, you qualify if you are on a low income, so that you get the item at reduced cost. Whether or not you qualify depends on your circumstances, including how much income you have.

How do you claim?

Ask at your dentist, optician or hospital about exemption. If you are in an exempt group, you are usually asked to complete the back of the prescription form or to complete another appropriate form. If you are not exempt, claim help under the low income scheme on Form HC1, available from GP practices, dentists, opticians, some chemists and advice centres, or apply online at services.nhsbsa.nhs.uk/apply-for-help-with-nhs-costs/apply-online.

Healthy Start and Best Start foods

Healthy Start (in England and Wales) and Best Start foods (in Scotland) can help towards your food shopping cost if you are pregnant or have a young child.

Health Start provides weekly vouchers to spend on milk, plain fresh and frozen fruit and vegetables, and infant formula milk. You can also get free vitamins.

Best Start foods provides a payment card for milk, eggs, fresh, frozen or tinned fruit and vegetables and fresh or tinned pulses.

Who can claim?

You qualify for Healthy Start if the following apply.

- You are at least 10 weeks pregnant or you have a child aged under four.
- If you are aged 18 or over, you or a member of your family get income support, income-based jobseeker's allowance, income-related employment and support allowance or, depending on your income, universal credit or child tax credit. If you are under 18 and pregnant, you qualify even if you do not get any of these benefits.

You qualify for Best Start foods if the following apply.

- You are pregnant or resposible for a child under three.

- If you are aged 18 or over and get income support, income-based jobseeker's allowance, income-related employment and support allowance or pension credit or, depending on your income, universal credit, housing benefit or tax credits.

How much do you get?

Healthy Start: £3.10 a week during pregnancy, £6.20 a week per child aged under one and £3.10 per child aged one to three.

Best Start foods: £4.25 a week during pregnancy, £8.50 a week per child aged under one and £4.25 a week per child aged one or two.

How do you claim?

For Healthy Start, claim on the form in the Healthy Start leaflet (HS01) available from midwives, health visitors, maternity clinics and doctors' surgeries, or by phoning 0345 607 6823. Alternatively, download a form or access a form at healthystart.nhs.uk/healthy-start-vouchers/how-to-apply.

For Best Start foods, claim on the form (online or downloadable) at mygov.scot/best-start-grant-best-start-foods, or by phoning 0800 182 2222.

Housing benefit

Housing benefit is for people on a low income who need help paying their rent. It is paid by your local authority. Your entitlement is affected by your income and capital, but you do not need to have paid national insurance contributions.

Housing benefit is being replaced by universal credit. If you come under the universal credit system, you cannot make a new claim for housing benefit unless you have reached 'pension age'. At some point, people already getting housing benefit will be transferred to universal credit.

Who can claim?

You can only make a new claim for housing benefit in the following limited circumstances.

- You (or your current partner) are getting or have recently been getting an extra amount for severe disability (a 'severe disability premium') in another means-tested benefit. This rule is currently due to end on 27 January 2021.

- You are at least 'pension age'. If you are in a couple, usually both you and your partner must be of pension age. If one of you is below pension age, usually you cannot make a new claim for housing benefit, unless you were at least pension age on 14 May 2019 and were entitled as a couple to pension credit or housing benefit (or both) and are still entitled to one or both of those benefits as part of the same couple.

- You are in certain accommodation ('specified' or 'temporary' accommodation) where you get care, support or supervision, or because you left your home due to domestic violence, or you are in homeless accommodation.

You qualify if all of the following apply.

- You do not come under the universal credit system.
- You or your partner are liable to pay rent for your home.
- You are not excluded from entitlement. Most full-time students cannot get housing benefit, although lone parents, some couples with children and students with disabilities can. People living in care homes and those considered not to be renting on a commercial basis are also excluded.
- You satisfy the 'habitual residence test' and the 'right to reside test', and are not a 'person subject to immigration control'.
- You do not have more than £16,000 capital (unless you also get the 'guarantee credit' of pension credit) and your income is sufficiently low.

How much do you get?

The local authority calculates your entitlement. In the calculation, basic amounts are included for you, your partner and your children. An amount cannot be included for a third or subsequent child if s/he was born on or after 6 April 2017, unless an exception applies and s/he is included in your child tax credit.

The actual amount you get depends on your circumstances – including the amount of your rent, your income and capital (including your partner's income and capital), and whether anyone else is living in your home. The local authority also takes into account the size of your property and how many bedrooms you have – see lha-direct.voa.gov.uk/bedroomcalculator.aspx. The Department for Work and Pensions provides links to independent benefit calculators at gov.uk/benefits-calculators.

If the total amount of benefit you get is limited by the 'benefit cap', the cap is applied by reducing the amount of housing benefit you get. There is an official calculator to estimate the level at which your benefit could be capped at gov.uk/benefit-cap-calculator.

Income support

Income support is a benefit paid by the Department for Work and Pensions to certain groups of people who are on a low income and who are not looking for work – eg, some lone parents and carers. Your entitlement is affected by your income and capital, but you do not need to have paid national insurance contributions.

Income support is being replaced by universal credit. If you come under the universal credit system, you cannot make a new claim for income support. At some point, people already getting income support will be transferred to universal credit.

Who can claim?

Usually you can only make a new claim for income support if you (or your current partner) are getting or have recently been getting an extra amount for severe disability (a 'severe disability premium') in another 'means-tested benefit'. This rule is currently due to end on 27 January 2021.

You qualify for income support if all of the following apply.

- You do not come under the universal credit system.
- You are aged at least 16 and are under 'pension age'.
- You are in one of the groups of people who can claim income support.
- You are not working for more than 16 hours a week, and your partner is not working for more than 24 hours a week.
- You are not entitled to jobseeker's allowance and your partner is not entitled to income-based jobseeker's allowance or pension credit.

- You are not entitled to employment and support allowance and your partner is not entitled to income-related employment and support allowance.
- You are in Great Britain, satisfy the 'habitual residence test' and the 'right to reside test', and are not a 'person subject to immigration control'.
- You do not have more than £16,000 capital and your income is sufficiently low.

You are in a group who can qualify for income support if one of the following applies.

- You are a lone parent with a child aged under five (or a child of any age if you are under 18).
- You get carer's allowance, or you care for a disabled person who:
  - gets attendance allowance
  - gets the highest or middle rate of the 'care component' of disability living allowance
  - gets either rate of the 'daily living component' of personal independence payment
  - has claimed one of these benefits in the last 26 weeks and is waiting for a decision
- You are pregnant and there are 11 weeks or less before the baby is due, or you are incapable of work because of the pregnancy, or you gave birth not more than 15 weeks ago.
- You are a lone foster parent of a child under 16, a 'kinship carer', or a single parent of a child under 16 placed with you for adoption.
- You get statutory sick pay or, in some cases, you are on parental or paternity leave from work, are not entitled to any payments from your employer and you were getting tax credits before your leave began.
- You are a young person in full-time, 'non-advanced education' (eg, at school or college), or you are an orphan with no one acting in place of your parents, or you are living away from your parents in certain circumstances, including if you are estranged.
- You are looking after a partner or child who is temporarily ill.

- You are in a specified special situation, including if you are a refugee learning English in order to get employment or you are not at work because of a trade dispute.

How much do you get?

The Department for Work and Pensions calculates your entitlement. In the calculation, basic amounts are included for you and your partner. Amounts for children are not included.

The actual amount you get depends on your circumstances – including whether you have a severe disability or you are a carer, as well as the amount of your income and capital. The circumstances (including the income and capital) of your partner are also taken into account. The Department for Work and Pensions provides links to independent benefit calculators at gov.uk/benefits-calculators.

How do you claim?

Claim by phoning 0800 169 0350 (Relay UK dial 18001 first; textphone 0800 023 4888). Alternatively, you can download a form from gov.uk/income-support/how-to-claim.

Industrial injuries benefits

Industrial injuries benefits are paid by the Department for Work and Pensions to people who are disabled as a result of an accident at work or an industrial disease. The main benefit is **industrial injuries disablement benefit**. If you were disabled by the accident or disease before 1 October 1990, you may be able to get **reduced earnings allowance**. People who have reached 'pension age' and were entitled to reduced earnings allowance may be able to get **retirement allowance**.

Industrial injuries benefits are not affected by your income or capital, and you do not have to have paid national insurance contributions.

Who can claim?

You qualify if all of the following apply.

- You have had a personal injury in an accident at work, or you have a prescribed industrial disease.
- At the time of the injury you were an employee, or your disease was caused by your work as an employee.
- As a result of that injury or disease, you are assessed as having a sufficient level of disablement.

More official information is available at gov.uk/industrial-injuries-disablement-benefit.

How much do you get?

You get industrial injuries benefit for yourself. Amounts for your partner and children are not included. The amount you get depends on the extent of your disablement.

How do you claim?

Request a claim form by phoning 0800 121 8379 (Relay UK dial 18001 first; textphone 0800 169 0314) or download a form from gov.uk/industrial-injuries-disablement-benefit/how-to-claim.

Jobseeker's allowance

Jobseeker's allowance is a benefit paid by the Department for Work and Pensions to people who are unemployed or working few hours, and who meet certain responsibilities about looking for work. The Department for Work and Pensions calls these 'jobseeking conditions'.

There are two types of jobseeker's allowance: income-based and contribution-based. You can be entitled to both. However, income-based jobseeker's allowance is being replaced by universal credit and, in most cases, you cannot make a new claim for it.

Income-based jobseeker's allowance

Income-based jobseeker's allowance is for people looking for work and on a low income. Your entitlement is affected by your income and capital, but you do not need to have paid national insurance contributions.

Income-based jobseeker's allowance is being replaced by universal credit. If you come under the universal credit system, you cannot make a new claim for income-based jobseeker's allowance. At some point, people already getting income-based jobseeker's allowance will be transferred to universal credit.

Who can claim?

You can only make a new claim if you (or your current partner) are getting or have recently been getting an extra amount for severe disability (a 'severe disability premium') in another 'means-tested benefit'. This rule is currently due to end on 27 January 2021. Otherwise, if you make a new claim for any kind of jobseeker's allowance, you cannot get income-based jobseeker's allowance.

You qualify if all of the following apply.

- You do not come under the universal credit system.
- You are aged at least 18 and under 'pension age'. Some 16/17-year-olds can qualify if they are in a couple and have a child; if not, they can apply for a severe hardship payment of income-based jobseeker's allowance.
- You are unemployed or are working less than 16 hours a week, and your partner is unemployed or working less than 24 hours a week.
- You satisfy the 'jobseeking conditions' – ie, you must be available for and actively seeking work.
- You are not getting income support, income-related employment and support allowance or pension credit.
- Your partner is not getting income support, income-based jobseeker's allowance, income-related employment and support allowance or pension credit.
- Usually, you must not be in full-time education. However, you can qualify during the summer holidays if you are a lone parent

or if you and your partner are both full-time students and have a child.

- You do not have more than £16,000 capital and your income is sufficiently low.
- You are in Great Britain, satisfy the 'habitual residence test' and the 'right to reside test', and you are not a 'person subject to immigration control'.

How much do you get?

The Department for Work and Pensions calculates your entitlement. In the calculation, basic amounts are included for you and your partner. Amounts for children are not included.

The actual amount you get depends on your circumstances – including whether you have a severe disability or are a carer, and the amount of your income and capital. The circumstances (including the income and capital) of your partner are also taken into account. The Department for Work and Pensions provides links to independent benefit calculators at gov.uk/benefits-calculators.

How do you claim?

Claim income-based jobseeker's allowance by phoning a Jobcentre Plus contact centre on 0800 055 6688 (Relay UK dial 18001 first; textphone 0800 023 4888).

If you are already getting 'old-style' contribution-based jobseeker's allowance, you may not need to make a new claim for income-based jobseeker's allowance.

Contribution-based jobseeker's allowance

Contribution-based jobseeker's allowance is for people looking for work who have paid sufficient national insurance contributions to qualify. It is not affected by your capital or by your income, other than your earnings or any occupational or personal pension you have. Your earnings are taken into account in full, except for a disregard of usually £5 a week. The first £50 a week of your occupational or personal pension is ignored, but amounts above that are taken into account.

Contribution-based jobseeker's allowance is not being replaced by universal credit. So you can get it at the same time as getting universal credit, in which case the Department for Work and Pensions calls it 'new-style' contribution-based jobseeker's allowance. If you do not come under the universal credit system, you can get it topped up with income-based jobseeker's allowance instead, in which case the Department for Work and Pensions calls it 'old-style' contribution-based jobseeker's allowance. If you are getting 'old-style' contribution-based jobseeker's allowance, you can get it topped up with income-based jobseeker's allowance without having to make a new claim – your current award can be adjusted to include the income-based form.

Who can claim?
You qualify if all of the following apply.

- You are unemployed or are working less than 16 hours a week.
- You do not have 'limited capability for work' – ie, you are not considered too ill to work.
- You satisfy the 'jobseeking conditions' – ie, you must be available for and actively seeking work. If you come under the universal credit system, you must satisfy the work-related requirements.
- You satisfy the national insurance contribution conditions. These include having paid sufficient class 1 or class 2 contributions in one of the last two recent tax years before the year of your claim, so you need to have been working at least at some point in those years.
- You are under 'pension age'.
- You are not getting income support.
- You are in Great Britain.

How much do you get?
You get an amount for yourself. Amounts for your partner and children are not included. The amount depends on your age.

Under 25: £58.90 a week.

25 or over: £74.35 a week.

How do you claim?

Claim 'new-style' contribution-based jobseeker's allowance at gov.uk/
jobseekers-allowance/apply-new-style-jsa. If you need help or cannot
claim online, claim by phoning Jobcentre Plus on 0800 055 6688
(Relay UK dial 18001 first; textphone 0800 023 4888).

If you do not come under the universal credit system, you can claim
'old-style' contribution-based jobseeker's allowance in the same way
as you would claim income-based jobseeker's allowance.

Local welfare assistance

Local authorities can pay local welfare assistance to people in need –
eg, to ease exceptional pressure on a family or following a crisis.
These may be in the form of a grant or a loan. In England, local
authorities have the discretion to make their own rules. In Scotland,
the Scottish Welfare Fund, paid through your local authority, provides
grants, vouchers or goods. In Wales, the Discretionary Assistance
Fund for Wales, paid through your local authority, also offers non-
repayable payments.

How do you claim?

Contact your local authority. It will advise you what its claim
procedures are.

Maternity allowance

Maternity allowance is a benefit paid by the Department for Work
and Pensions to women who are pregnant or who have recently
given birth and who are not entitled to statutory maternity pay. It is
not affected by your income or capital, and you do not need to have
paid national insurance contributions.

Who can claim?

You qualify if all of the following apply.

- You are pregnant or have recently given birth and are within your 'maternity allowance period'. This is a period of 39 weeks (in some cases, 14 weeks) starting, at the earliest, 11 weeks before the week in which your baby is due.
- You were working for at least 26 weeks in the 66 weeks immediately before the week in which your baby is due, or you assisted your spouse or civil partner with her/his self-employment in at least 26 weeks of those 66 weeks (in this case, your maternity allowance period is 14 weeks rather than 39).
- Your average gross earnings in the 66 weeks immediately before the week in which your baby is due were at least £30 a week (if you were working).
- You are not entitled to statutory maternity pay.

There is an official calculator for working out your eligibility at gov.uk/pay-leave-for-parents.

How much do you get?

You get either 90 per cent of your average weekly earnings, or £151.20 a week, whichever is less. If you qualify because you help with your spouse or civil partner's self-employment, you get £27 a week.

How do you claim?

Claim on Form MA1, available from the Department for Work and Pensions on 0800 055 6688 (textphone 0800 023 4888) or from gov.uk/maternity-allowance/how-to-claim.

Pension credit

Pension credit is a benefit paid by the Department for Work and Pensions to people who have reached 'pension age' and who are on a low income. Your entitlement is affected by your income, but you do not need to have paid national insurance contributions.

Pension credit has two elements. A 'guarantee credit', which brings your income up to a minimum level, and a 'savings credit'. This is for people aged over 65 who reached pension age before 6 April 2016 and whose income is at least a certain level. Savings credit is being phased out and you cannot now qualify for it for the first time.

Who can claim?

You qualify for the guarantee credit of pension credit if all of the following apply.

- You have reached 'pension age'.
- Your income is low enough.
- Your partner is not already entitled to pension credit. If your partner has not reached pension age, see below.
- You are in Great Britain, you satisfy the 'habitual residence test' and the 'right to reside test', and you are not a 'person subject to immigration control'.

You can check your pension age at gov.uk/state-pension-age.

If your partner has not reached pension age, usually you cannot make a new claim for pension credit, unless on 14 May 2019 you were, as part of the same couple, entitled to pension credit or housing benefit for people of pension age (or both), and are still entitled to one or both of those benefits as part of the same couple.

How much do you get?

The Department for Work and Pensions calculates your entitlement. In the calculation, basic amounts are included for you, your partner and dependant children.

The actual amount you get depends on your circumstances – including whether you have a severe disability or you are a carer, your income and (if you have capital of over £10,000) your capital.

The circumstances (including the income and capital) of your partner are also taken into account. There is an official calculator for working out how much you might get at gov.uk/pension-credit/what-youll-get.

How do you claim?

The Department for Work and Pensions encourages you to start your claim by phoning the Pension Service on 0800 991 234 (textphone 0800 169 0133). Alternatively, you can use the claim form, Form PC1, which you can get from the Pension Service. In some circumstances, you can also claim at gov.uk/pension-credit/how-to-claim.

Personal independence payment

Personal independence is a benefit paid by the Department for Work and Pensions to people aged between 16 and 'pension age' who have care needs and/or have mobility problems because of a disability. Your entitlement is not affected by your income or capital, and you do not have to have paid national insurance contributions.

Personal independence payment has replaced disability living allowance. Those already getting disability living allowance are having their awards transferred to personal independence payment. People over pension age who are claiming for the first time must claim attendance allowance instead.

Who can claim?

You qualify if all of the following apply.

- You are aged between 16 and 'pension age'.
- You satisfy certain conditions about residence and presence in the UK and are not a 'person subject to immigration control'.
- You satisfy a disability test.

Personal independence payment has two components: one for problems with daily living activities, such as preparing food, washing and bathing, communicating and engaging with other people; and one for mobility activities, including planning and following journeys and moving around. You can receive one or both. You are given a certain number of points for the severity of your problems in each activity. You can get different rates of each component, depending on how many points you score.

How much do you get?

Daily living component:

Standard rate: £59.70 a week.

Enhanced rate: £89.15 a week.

Mobility component:

Standard rate: £23.60 a week.

Enhanced rate: £62.25 a week.

How do you claim?

Start your claim by phoning the personal independence payment claim line on 0800 917 2222 (Relay UK dial 18001 first; textphone 0800 917 7777). A 'How your disability affects you' form is then sent to you. A video relay service is available for British Sign Language users at gov.uk/pip/how-to-claim. Different arrangements apply if you are unable to claim by telephone or are terminally ill: see gov.uk/pip/how-to-claim.

Scottish child payment

Scottish child payment is being introduced for families living in Scotland, to top up 'means-tested benefits'. Payments are due to begin in February 2021. Initially, it will be paid for children aged under six. The Scottish Government plans to extend this to children under 16 by the end of 2022.

Who can claim?

At the time this book was written, the detailed rules had not been finalised. It was expected that you will qualify if all of the following apply.

- You live in Scotland.
- You are responsible for a child aged under six.
- You or your partner are entitled to one or more of the following 'qualifying benefits':
  - universal credit
  - income support
  - income-based jobseeker's allowance
  - income-related employment and support allowance
  - child tax credit
  - working tax credit
  - pension credit

You count as responsible for a child if you or your partner get child benefit for her/him, or an amount for her/him is included in your universal credit, child tax credit or pension credit, or you are her/his kinship carer.

How much do you get?

£10 a week for each child who qualifies.

How do you claim?

Claim at mygov.scot/benefits or by phoning 0800 182 222.

Social fund payments

The social fund is made up of a number of payments that can be made by the Department for Work and Pensions to people on a low income in certain situations, including following the birth of a baby. These are **budgeting loans**, **Sure Start maternity grants** (England and Wales only), **funeral expenses payments** (England and Wales only), winter fuel payments and cold weather payments. Some payments require you to be getting a qualifying benefit in order to qualify.

In Scotland, Sure Start maternity grants are replaced under the Best Start grants scheme and funeral expenses payments are replaced by funeral support payments.

Who can claim?

Budgeting loans are for specified types of expenses, such as an item of furniture or household equipment. They are discretionary, so a loan is not guaranteed. You must have been getting one of the following qualifying benefits for at least 26 weeks:

- income support
- income-based jobseeker's allowance
- income-related employment and support allowance
- pension credit

The amount paid is determined by a formula based on the size of your family and the amount of any outstanding budgeting loan debt you may already have. Loans are repaid through weekly deductions from benefits, but are interest free. The loan must be repaid within 104 weeks. **Note:** if you are getting universal credit, you cannot apply for a budgeting loan and must apply for a 'budgeting advance' of your universal credit instead.

A **Sure Start maternity grant** is a £500 lump sum payable to people on a low income to help with the costs of a new baby. If you are already getting a grant for another child under 16, you cannot get the grant. You must be getting one of the following qualifying benefits:

- universal credit
- income support
- income-based jobseeker's allowance
- income-related employment and support allowance
- pension credit
- child tax credit of more than just the family element
- working tax credit including the disabled worker or severe disability element

The grant must be claimed within three months of the baby's birth (or an adoption or residence or parental order).

A **funeral expenses payment** is a lump sum to cover the basic costs of a funeral plus some other related expenses. You must be responsible for the funeral arrangements and be getting one of the following qualifying benefits:

- universal credit
- income support
- income-based jobseeker's allowance
- income-related employment and support allowance
- housing benefit
- pension credit
- child tax credit of more than just the family element
- working tax credit including the disabled worker or severe disability element

The payment may be recovered from any money or assets left by the person who died. There are also rules that exclude some people from claiming if someone else, not on benefit, could have paid for the funeral. In addition, in England there is a **children's funeral payment** to cover the 'reasonable' costs of a funeral of a child aged under 18 or a stillborn child born after the 24th week of pregnancy. A children's funeral payment is applied for by the person providing the funeral – ie, the funeral director in most cases.

A **winter fuel payment** is a lump-sum payment to help pay fuel bills, although it can be spent on anything. You must be at least 'pension age' to qualify. It is usually paid automatically, but if you are over pension age and not on any benefits, you may have to make a claim as the Department for Work and Pensions may not know you are entitled to a payment.

Cold weather payments are paid to people getting one of the following qualifying benefits during recorded periods of cold weather:

- universal credit
- income support
- income-based jobseeker's allowance

- income-related employment and support allowance
- pension credit

Note: there are other qualifying conditions.

In some cases, you can claim a social fund payment if your partner has an award of the qualifying benefit or tax credit.

How do you claim?

Apply for a budgeting loan at gov.uk/budgeting-help-benefits/how-to-claim, or use Form SF500, which you can get by phoning your local job centre or the social fund on 0800 169 0140 (Relay UK dial 18001 first; textphone 0800 169 286).

Apply for a Sure Start maternity grant on Form SF100, which you can get from your local job centre or from gov.uk/sure-start-maternity-grant/how-to-claim.

Start your claim for a funeral payment by phoning the Bereavement Service on 0800 731 0469 (textphone 0800 731 0464). Form SF200 is then sent to you. You can also download the form from gov.uk/funeral-payments/how-to-claim.

You should automatically receive a winter fuel payment without needing to claim if you got one in the previous year, or if you are getting a retirement pension or another benefit. Otherwise, you contact the winter fuel payment helpline on 0800 731 0160 (textphone 0800 731 0176).

You do not need to make a claim for cold weather payments. The Department for Work and Pensions pays you automatically if you qualify.

Statutory adoption pay

Statutory adoption pay is paid by employers to their employees who are stopping work to adopt a child and who satisfy certain conditions about employment and earnings. Your entitlement is not affected by your income and capital.

Who can claim?

You qualify if all of the following apply.

- You are adopting a child.
- You have worked for your employer continuously for at least 26 weeks by the time you were matched with the child for adoption.
- Your average gross earnings are at least a certain level, currently £120 a week.
- You give the correct notice and proof of the adoption to your employer.
- You are in the 'adoption pay period' – this is 39 weeks, usually beginning, at the earliest, 14 days before the day you expect the child to be placed with you and, at the latest, on the date of placement.

Official information about the notice and proof is available at gov.uk/adoption-pay-leave/eligibility.

How much do you get?

First six weeks: 90 per cent of your average weekly earnings a week.

Remaining 33 weeks: £151.20 a week (or 90 per cent of your average weekly earnings, if less).

How do you claim?

Contact your employer. There is no claim form, but you must give your employer the correct notice and information.

Statutory maternity pay

Statutory maternity pay is paid by employers to their employees who are stopping work to have a baby, and who satisfy certain conditions about employment and earnings. Your entitlement is not affected by your income and capital.

Who can claim?

You qualify if all of the following apply.

- You are pregnant or have recently given birth.
- You have worked for your employer continuously for at least 26 weeks by the 15th week before the week in which your baby is due.
- Your average gross earnings are at least a certain level, currently £120 a week.
- You give the correct notice and proof of the pregnancy to your employer.
- You are in the 'maternity pay period' – this is 39 weeks beginning, at the earliest, 11 weeks before the week in which your baby is due and, at the latest, the day after your baby is born.

Official information about the notice and proof is available at gov.uk/maternity-pay-leave/how-to-claim.

How much do you get?

First six weeks: 90 per cent of your average weekly earnings a week.

Remaining 33 weeks: £151.20 a week (or 90 per cent of your average weekly earnings, if less).

How do you claim?

Contact your employer. There is no claim form, but you must give your employer the correct notice and information.

Statutory parental bereavement pay

Statutory parental bereavement pay is paid by employers to employees who meet certain conditions after the death of a child or a stillbirth. It is paid for up to two weeks.

Who can claim

You qualify if all of the following apply.

- You are a bereaved parent following the death of a child aged under 18 or following a stillbirth after 24 weeks of pregnancy.
- You have been continuously employed by the same employer for at least 26 weeks up to the week in which the child died or was stillborn.
- Your average gross earnings are at least a certain level, currently £120 a week.
- You give your employer correct notice of the week or weeks you want the payment to be made.

Official information about correct notice and other matters is available at gov.uk/parental-bereavement-pay-leave/how-to-claim.

How much do you get?

£151.20 a week (or 90 per cent of your average weekly earnings, if less).

How do you claim?

Contact your employer. There is no claim form, but you must give your employer the correct notice and information.

Statutory paternity pay

Statutory paternity pay is paid by employers to certain employees who are taking time off work to care for a child. Your entitlement is not affected by your income or capital.

Who can claim?

You qualify if all of the following apply.

- You are the father, the husband or partner of the mother (or the adopter of the child), the child's adopter or the intended parent if you are having a baby through a surrogacy arrangement.
- You have worked for your employer continuously for at least 26 weeks by the 15th week before the baby is due.
- You are employed by your employer up to the date of birth.
- Your average gross earnings are at least a certain level, currently £120 week.
- You give the correct notice to your employer.
- You are in the 'statutory paternity pay period' – this is a maximum of two consecutive weeks. The earliest date that statutory paternity pay can be paid from is the child's date of birth (or the date of her/his placement for adoption) and the latest is eight weeks after this date.

Official information about the notice is available at gov.uk/paternity-pay-leave/how-to-claim.

How much do you get?

£151.20 (or 90 per cent of your average weekly earnings, if less).

How do you claim?

Contact your employer. There is no claim form, but you must give your employer the correct notice.

Statutory shared parental pay

Statutory shared parental pay is paid by an employer to an employee whose partner has given up her statutory maternity pay, maternity allowance or statutory adoption pay early. The remaining pay can be paid to the mother's partner as statutory shared parental pay to enable both partners to stop work and care for the child. You can be paid for a maximum of 37 weeks.

Who can claim?

You qualify if all of the following apply.

- You are the child's mother or father, or the mother's partner.
- The mother has given up her statutory maternity allowance, maternity allowance or statutory adoption pay early.
- You have worked for your employer continuously for at least 26 weeks by the 15th week before the baby is due (or in adoption cases, the week in which you were notified of being matched with a child).
- Your average gross earnings are at least a certain level, currently £120 a week.
- Your partner (or if s/he is not your partner, the other parent or the adopter) has been employed or self-employed for 26 weeks in the 66 weeks up to the week before the baby is due (or in adoption cases, the week in which the adopter was notified of the match).
- Your partner (or if s/he is not your partner, the other parent or the adopter) had average earnings of at least £30 a week in 13 weeks out of the above 66-week period.
- You give the correct notice and information to your employer.

Official information about the notice and information is available at gov.uk/shared-parental-leave-and-pay/applying-for-leave-and-pay.

How much do you get?

£151.20 a week (or 90 per cent of your average weekly earnings, if less).

How do you claim?

Contact your employer. There is no claim form, but you must give your employer the correct notice and information.

Tax credits

Tax credits are paid by HM Revenue and Customs to people with children and/or who are working, and on a low income. Your entitlement is affected by your income, but you do not have to have paid national insurance contributions.

There are two types of tax credits: **child tax credit** and **working tax credit**. You can get either or both, depending on your circumstances.

Tax credits are being replaced by universal credit. If you come under the universal credit system, you cannot make a completely new claim for tax credits. At some point, people already getting tax credits will be transferred to universal credit.

Child tax credit

Child tax credit can be paid if you have a child and are on a low income, whether you are working or not.

Who can claim?

Usually you can only make a new claim for child tax credit if you (or your current partner) are getting or have recently been getting an extra amount for severe disability (a 'severe disability premium') in another 'means-tested benefit'. This rule is currently due to end on 27 January 2021. Note that you can start to get child tax credit if you are already getting working tax credit without having to make a new claim for tax credits. Also, you can renew an existing award at the end of the tax year.

You qualify for child tax credit if all of the following apply.

- You do not come under the universal credit system.
- You are aged 16 or over.
- You are responsible for a child. This includes all children aged under 16, and young people aged 16 to 19 who are in 'non-advanced education' at school or college (eg, studying GCSEs, AS and A levels, NVQ level 3 or below, Scottish National Qualifications up to Higher or Advanced Higher level or for a

BTEC) for more than 12 hours a week, or those aged 16 to 19 in approved training.
- Your income is low enough.
- You are present and ordinarily resident in the UK, you satisfy the 'right to reside test' and you are not a 'person subject to immigration control'.

How much do you get?

HM Revenue and Customs calculates your entitlement. In the calculation, basic amounts for yourself and your family are included. Amounts for up to at least two children are also included. An amount cannot be included for a third or subsequent child if s/he was born on or after 6 April 2017, unless one of the following applies.

- The child was the second or subsequent child in a multiple birth.
- The child is living with you because s/he is unable to live with her/his parents and either there is a child arrangements order, you are her/his legal guardian or 'kinship carer' or it is likely that the child would have to go into local authority care if s/he were not living with you.
- You have adopted the child from a local authority.
- It is likely that the child was born as the result of rape, or in a controlling or coercive relationship.
- The child's parent is a child for whom you are responsible.

The actual amount you get depends on your circumstances. This includes whether all your children were born on or after 6 April 2017, whether you have a child with a disability, and the amount of your income (your partner's income is also taken into account). An official calculator for estimating how much you might get is available at gov.uk/tax-credits-calculator.

How do you claim?

Child tax credit and working tax credit can both be claimed by phoning the Tax Credit Helpline on 0345 300 3900 (textphone 0345 300 3909).

Working tax credit

Working tax credit can be paid if you are working at least 16 hours a week (or in some cases, 24 or 30 hours) and have a low income.

Who can claim?

Usually you can only make a new claim for working tax credit if you (or your current partner) are getting or have recently been getting an extra amount for severe disability (a 'severe disability premium') in another 'means-tested benefit'. This rule is currently due to end on 27 January 2021. Note that you can start to get working tax credit if you are already getting child tax credit without having to make a new claim for tax credits. Also, you can renew an existing award at the end of the tax year.

You qualify if all of the following apply.

- You do not come under the universal credit system.
- You are at least 16 years old.
- You (or your partner) are in full-time work.
- Your income is low enough.
- You are present and ordinarily resident in the UK, and you are not a 'person subject to immigration control'.

You count as being in full-time work if one of the following applies.

- You work at least 30 hours a week and you are aged 25 or over.
- You are in a couple, your combined hours of work are at least 24 hours a week, and you have a child. One of you must work at least 16 hours a week, so if only one of you works, it must be for at least 24 hours a week.
- You work at least 16 hours a week and:
  - you are single and have a child
  - you are a member of a couple, you have a child and your partner is incapacitated, entitled to carer's allowance, or is in hospital or prison
  - you are disabled
  - you are aged 60 or over

You are treated as being in full-time work while you are getting statutory sick pay, statutory maternity pay, statutory adoption pay, statutory paternity pay, statutory shared parental pay, statutory parental bereavement pay or maternity allowance. You are also treated as being in full-time work if you were in full-time work before getting employment and support allowance or income support while incapable of work due to pregnancy.

How much do you get?
HM Revenue and Customs calculates your entitlement. The actual amount you get depends on your circumstances. In the calculation, you get basic amounts plus additional amounts if you are a lone parent or in a couple, if you work at least 30 hours a week, or if you have a disability or are severely disabled. You also get an amount included for the cost of your childcare.

HM Revenue and Customs also takes into account your income and your partner's income, including earnings. An official calculator for estimating how much you might get is available at gov.uk/tax-credits-calculator.

How do you claim?
Working tax credit and child tax credit can both be claimed by phoning the Tax Credit Helpline on 0345 300 3900 (textphone 0345 300 3909).

Universal credit

Universal credit is a benefit paid by the Department for Work and Pensions to people who come under the universal credit system and who are on a low income. Your entitlement is affected by your income and capital, but you do not need to have paid national insurance contributions. Universal credit can be paid to you whether you are in or out of work, and whether or not you are able to work.

When do you come under the universal credit system?

You come under the universal credit system if you make a claim for universal credit. If you make a claim for universal credit, any entitlement you or your partner has to income support, income-based jobseeker's allowance, income-related employment and support allowance, housing benefit (except if you are in certain 'specified' or temporary accommodation, such as a domestic violence refuge or certain accommodation where you get support or supervision) and tax credits will stop, even if it turns out that you are not entitled to universal credit because you have too much income or capital. In most cases, you cannot make a new claim for those benefits, whether or not you have already claimed universal credit. The exception is if you are prevented by law from claiming universal credit, and so cannot come under the universal credit system. This is where you (or your current partner) are getting or have recently been getting an extra amount for severe disability (a 'severe disability premium') in another 'means-tested benefit'. This rule is currently due to end on 27 January 2021.

If you make a new claim for employment and support allowance or jobseeker's allowance (of any kind), in most cases you come under the universal credit system. This means that you cannot get income-related employment and support allowance or income-based jobseeker's allowance. The exception is if you are prevented by law from claiming universal credit, and so cannot come under the universal credit system.

At some point, the Department for Work and Pensions will begin transferring people getting income support, income-based jobseeker's allowance, income-related employment and support allowance, housing benefit and tax credits to universal credit.

Who can claim?

You qualify if all of the following conditions are met.

- You come under the universal credit system.
- You are at least 18, but under 'pension age'. Some 16/17-year-olds who have a child or are pregnant can also claim.
- You are not receiving education. Some exceptions apply, including if you have a child or are a foster parent, or your partner is not receiving education.

- You satisfy the 'habitual residence test' and the 'right to reside test', and you not a 'person subject to immigration control'.
- You have accepted a 'claimant commitment'.
- You do not have £16,000 or more in capital, and your income is low enough.

If you are a member of a couple, you make a joint claim and usually your partner must also satisfy the above conditions, although there are exceptions, including where your partner has reached pension age.

How much do you get?

The Department for Work and Pensions calculates your entitlement. In the calculation, basic amounts for yourself and your family are included. However, an amount cannot be included for a third or subsequent child who becomes part of your family on or after 6 April 2017, unless one of the following applies.

- The child was the second or subsequent child in a multiple birth.
- The child is living with you because s/he is unable to live with her/his parents and either there is a child arrangements order, you are her/his legal guardian or 'kinship carer' or it is likely that the child would have to go into local authority care if s/he were not living with you.
- You have adopted the child from a local authority.
- It is likely that the child was born as the result of rape, or in a controlling or coercive relationship.
- The child's parent is a child aged under 16 for whom you are responsible.

The actual amount you get depends on your circumstances – including whether you are able to work, whether you have a disabled child and whether you are a carer, and the amount of your income and capital. You also get an amount included for the cost of your childcare. The circumstances (including any income and capital) of your partner are also taken into account.

If you have correctly been allowed to claim universal credit but you (or your current partner) were getting an amount for severe disability (the 'severe disability premium') in an award of a 'means-tested benefit' before you claimed universal credit, you are entitled to an extra amount of universal credit, called the 'transitional SDP amount'. This is a lump sum included in your monthly payment, but does not guarantee that your universal credit is the same amount as your old means-tested benefit.

The Department for Work and Pensions provides links to independent benefit calculators at gov.uk/benefits-calculators.

How do you claim?

Universal credit must be claimed online. There is no paper claim form. To start your claim, go to gov.uk/apply-universal-credit.

If you need help claiming online, contact the official helpline on 0800 328 5644 (textphone 0800 328 1344). You can also get help making a claim from the Citizens Advice 'Help to Claim' service.

Young carer grant

Young carer grants are paid by Social Security Scotland to young people aged 16 to 18 living in Scotland who care for someone with a disability.

Who can claim?

You qualify if all of the following apply.

- You live in Scotland.
- You are aged at least 16 and under 19.
- You are caring (usually for an average of at least 16 hours a week) for a person who is receiving any of the following:
  - attendance allowance
  - either the highest or the middle rate of disability living allowance care component
  - either rate of the daily living component of personal independence payment

- armed forces independence payment
- constant attendance allowance with an industrial injury benefit or war pension.
- You are not entitled to carer's allowance.

How much do you get?

£305.10 paid as an annual payment.

How do you claim?

Claim at mygov.scot/young-carer-grant/how-to-apply, by phoning 0800 182 2222 or on the claim form which you can either download online or request on the phone.

Appendix

Glossary of terms

Advance
An advance payment of universal credit which can be paid if you are in hardship while waiting for a universal credit payment.

Applicable amount
An amount used to help calculate how much income support, income-based jobseeker's allowance, income-related employment and support allowance and housing benefit someone can get.

Appointee
Someone, often a relative, authorised by the Department for Work and Pensions to claim and receive benefit on another person's behalf if that person is either under 16 or cannot claim for her/himself – eg, because of a learning disability.

Assessment period
The monthly period on which payment of universal credit is based. You are paid up to seven days after the end of each assessment period.

Bedroom tax
A reduction in the amount of housing benefit or the housing costs element in universal credit affecting tenants of local authorities and housing associations who have a spare bedroom(s).

Benefit cap
The maximum amount of social security benefits that someone can receive. It includes most benefits, but there are some exceptions and some people to whom the cap does not apply.

Budgeting advance
A discretionary extra amount of universal credit to help with expenses, paid as a loan. You must usually have been on benefits for at least six months to qualify.

Capital
This includes savings, investments, certain lump-sum payments and property which is not a person's main home.

Care component
The part of disability living allowance paid if you need help looking after yourself or someone to keep an eye on you because of your disability or health problem.

Carer element
An extra amount of universal credit paid to people who care for a disabled child or adult.

Carer premium
An extra amount of income support, income-based jobseeker's allowance, income-related employment and support allowance or housing benefit paid to people who care for a disabled child or adult.

Child element
An amount for children included in a person's maximum universal credit or child tax credit award.

Childcare element
An extra amount in universal credit or working tax credit paid to people in work who pay for childcare.

Claimant commitment
A document setting out what you must do while claiming universal credit, and the possible penalties if its terms are not met.

Collect and pay
When the Child Maintenance Service collects money from the child's other parent and then pays you.

Contributory benefit
A benefit that requires the claimant to have paid, or been credited with, national insurance contributions in order to be entitled to it.

Daily living component
The part of personal independence payment paid if you have problems with daily living activities, or are terminally ill.

Determination
The term used by Social Security Scotland for a decision.

Disability premium
An extra amount of income support, income-based jobseeker's allowance and housing benefit paid to people getting personal independence payment or certain other benefits, or who are blind.

Disabled child addition
An extra amount of universal credit paid for a child or young person who gets disability living allowance or personal independence payment, or who is blind.

Disabled child premium
An extra amount of housing benefit paid for a child or young person who gets disability living allowance or personal independence payment, or who is blind.

Disabled worker element
An extra amount of working tax credit paid to someone with a disability.

Discretionary housing payment
A payment that can be made by a local authority to top up universal credit or housing benefit when someone in rented accommodation needs extra help with her/his housing costs.

Earnings threshold
The amount of a person's earnings (or joint earnings for couples) above which there is no expectation to look for more work, or meet any other work-related requirements for universal credit.

Elements
Amounts for children, disabilities, caring responsibilities, housing and childcare, which make up part of a person's maximum universal credit award.

Enhanced disability premium
An extra amount of income support, income-based jobseeker's allowance, employment and support allowance and housing benefit paid to people getting the enhanced rate of the daily living component of personal independence payment or the highest rate of the disability living allowance care component.

Family element
An amount included in the child tax credit calculation if the claim includes a child born before 6 April 2017.

Flexible Support Fund
A discretionary fund to help remove barriers to work, administered by local job centres.

Friend and family carer
A person who has taken responsibility for the child of a friend or relative under a formal caring arrangement, or an informal caring arrangement where it is likely the child would otherwise be looked after by the local authority. Sometimes referred to as a 'kinship carer'.

Grace period
A nine-month period when the benefit cap does not apply to your universal credit because your earnings in the last year were above a certain amount.

Guarantee credit
A type of pension credit for people whose income is below a certain level.

Habitual residence test
A test of whether someone has a settled intention to stay in the UK (or Republic of Ireland, Channel Islands or Isle of Man; for Best Start grant and young carer grant the UK, Channel Islands, Isle of Man or European Economic Area), and has usually been living here for a period.

Hardship payments
Reduced-rate payments of universal credit, jobseeker's allowance and employment and support allowance that are made in limited circumstances.

Healthcare professional
A doctor, nurse, paramedic, physiotherapist or occupational therapist who carries out assessments for disability benefits.

Housing costs element
The amount of universal credit that helps with rent and certain service charges.

Independent Case Examiner
A body handling complaints about the Department for Work and Pensions.

Interim payment
An amount of housing benefit or child benefit that may be paid when there is a delay in paying someone their full entitlement.

Jobseeker's agreement
A document used for jobseeker's allowance that sets out what someone must do to look for work. It is usually now referred to as a claimant commitment.

Jobseeking conditions
What you must do to be ready for work and to look for work in order to get jobseeker's allowance.

Kinship carer
A person who has taken responsibility for the child of a friend or relative under a formal caring arrangement, or an informal caring arrangement where it is likely the child would otherwise be looked after by the local authority. Sometimes referred to as a 'friend and family carer'.

Limited capability for work
A test of whether a person's ability to work is limited by a health condition.

Limited capability for work-related activity
A test of how severe a person's health problems are and whether her/his ability to prepare for work is limited.

Limited capability for work-related activity element
An extra amount of universal credit paid to people who are too ill to prepare for work or who have a severe disability.

Local housing allowance
The maximum amount of help with your rent if you live in private rented accommodation. Each local authority sets its own rate.

Local welfare assistance schemes
Run by local authorities to help people in need – eg, in a crisis or to ease exceptional pressure on a family.

Main carer
The person in a couple who spends the most time looking after the children, jointly nominated by the couple.

Mandatory reconsideration
The requirement to have a decision looked at again before an appeal can be made.

Mandatory reconsideration notice
The notice sent by the Department for Work and Pensions after someone makes a mandatory reconsideration request, which is needed in order to appeal.

Means-tested benefit
A benefit that is only paid if your income and capital are low enough, and which also considers the circumstances of your partner.

Minimum income floor
An amount based on the national minimum wage which self-employed people are assumed to have when their universal credit is worked out.

Mobility component
The part of disability living allowance or personal independence payment paid if you have mobility problems.

Motability
A scheme that allows you buy or lease a vehicle if you get the enhanced rate of the personal independence payment mobility component or the higher rate of the disability living allowance mobility component.

National minimum wage
A set minimum hourly rate that employers must pay. The government calls the rate for people aged 25 or over the national living wage.

Non-advanced education
Education below degree, Higher National Certificate or Higher National Diploma level, including national vocational qualification levels 1–3, GCSEs, A levels and Scottish Highers.

Non-dependant
An adult, other than a partner, who lives with the person claiming benefit – eg, a grown-up daughter or son.

Overpayment
An amount of benefit that is paid to you, which is more than your entitlement and which you may be asked to repay.

Pension age
The earliest age you can claim a state pension.

Person subject to immigration control
Someone who requires leave to enter or remain in the UK but does not have it, or who has leave to remain but is prohibited from having recourse to public funds, or has leave to remain in the UK on the basis of a sponsorship agreement.

Personal allowance
Part of the applicable amount. The amount varies, depending on your age and whether you are a single person or in a couple.

Premium
An extra amount of benefit paid with means-tested benefits, depending on your circumstances.

Qualifying child
A child who is under 16 or under 20 and in full-time non-advanced education and for whom you can get child maintenance.

Real-time information
A system whereby employers send HM Revenue and Customs information about employees' earnings every time they are paid, which is then used by the Department for Work and Pensions to adjust universal credit awards.

Redetermination
The requirement for Social Security Scotland benefits to have a decision looked at again before an appeal can be made.

Right to reside test
A social security test, mainly affecting European Economic Area nationals, which must be satisfied in order to claim certain benefits.

Sanction
A reduction in a person's benefit award for failing to meet certain work-related requirements.

Severe disability element
An extra amount of working tax credit paid if you get certain disability benefits.

Severe disability premium
An extra amount of means-tested benefits paid if you are getting the daily living component of personal independence payment, attendance allowance or the middle or highest rate of the disability living allowance care component, and you satisfy certain other conditions.

Short-term advance
An advance of benefit which can be paid if someone is in hardship while waiting for her/his first benefit payment.

Sign on
The requirement to attend a job centre and sign a declaration in order to get jobseeker's allowance.

Social Security Scotland
Agency which delivers social security benefits that are devolved to Scottish government.

Standard allowance
The basic amount of universal credit paid for a single adult or a couple.

Support component
An amount included in employment and support allowance for people who have limited capability for work-related activity.

Support group
Refers to people the Department for Work and Pensions has assessed as having limited capability for work-related activity.

Terminal illness
A progressive disease from which your death can reasonably be expected within six months.

Transitional SDP amount
An extra amount of universal credit, included where you (or your partner) were getting a severe disability premium in a means-tested benefit before claiming universal credit.

Two-child limit
A restriction on the number of child elements included in universal credit or child tax credit. There are exceptions – eg, if a child is adopted or for multiple births.

Variation
The process that enables someone to apply to the Child Maintenance Service to more accurately assess the income or circumstances of the paying parent.

Work allowance
The amount of earnings families and people who are ill or disabled are allowed to keep before their universal credit is affected.

Work availability
One of the work-related requirements, which means being willing and able to take up paid work, usually immediately and within 90 minutes' travel time of home.

Work capability assessment
A social security test used to decide whether someone is too ill to work.

Work coach
Someone employed by the Department for Work and Pensions to draw up claimant commitments, update them and check that people are meeting their work-related requirements.

Work-focused interview
A compulsory interview with the Department for Work and Pensions to discuss job opportunities, barriers to work and training.

Work preparation
One of the work-related requirements, which includes carrying out activities to prepare for a future return to work, such as increasing skills or doing a work placement.

Work-related activity
Activity that makes it more likely that someone will get a job or remain in work.

Work-related activity component
An amount included in employment and support allowance for people who have limited capability for work and whose claim started before 6 April 2017.

Work-related requirements
The activities that a person must undertake to continue to receive the full amount of universal credit.

Work search
One of the work-related requirements, which means normally spending 35 hours a week looking for work.

Index

W
winter fuel payment 188
winter heating assistance 102
work 76
  childcare costs 63
  financial help checklist 77
  ill health or disability 92
  looking after a child 78
  looking for work 79
  low-paid work 76, 79
  pregnant 23
working tax credit 197
  amount of benefit 198
  childcare costs 66
  having a baby 25
  how to claim 198
  rules about work and earnings 83
  who can claim 197

Y
young carer grant 201
  amount of benefit 202
  how to claim 202
  who can claim 201
young people
  non-advanced education 74
  school-leaving age 71
  young parents 38